Walking Winchester

explorations of the ancient city in

words by Bryan Dunleavy
and
drawings by Olena Thomas

WALKING WINCHESTER

Published by Magic Flute Publications 2014
ISBN 978-1-909054-24-0

Magic Flute Publications is an imprint of

Magic Flute Artworks Limited

231 Swanwick Lane

Southampton SO31 7GT

www.magicfluteartworks.com

A catalogue description of this book is available from the British Library

Contents

Index to Features

Introduction

Winchester was for a time one of England's most important cities. It is today one of its most historic and can tell a story covering at least 2000 years through its surviving buildings and ruins.

We have prepared this book to take you through that long period illustrating Winchester's highs and lows and encountering some of the people who not only left their mark on Winchester but also on England and Europe. We have chosen to do this through what is visible today. The drawings illustrate various aspects of the city that we believe are interesting and the commentary describes the history that is revealed through a building or ruin or fragment. It is not however a history of Winchester.

We have decided to illustrate the book with drawings rather than photographs. We believe that drawings are more expressive and we hope that through them some aspects of Winchester's personality will shine through. The choice of black and white is also deliberate. A colour photograph can be assessed in an instant; a black and white brush drawing may prompt closer attention. We are inviting you to look at Winchester more carefully.

The town was laid out by the Romans and the streets still follow that pattern. Once the Saxon kingdoms emerged Winchester became a royal town and because of the dominance of the kingdom of Wessex became for a time the capital of England. It was a location for royal palaces, a royal castle, the royal mint and several important religious houses and, not least, the seat of the richest bishop in England, the bishop of Winchester. It was a magnet for medieval England St Giles Hill used to annually host the largest international market in the country. Over time, the centre of political and commercial gravity shifted to London and other centres and by the 18th century Winchester had become a genteel provincial backwater, a state from which it recovered somewhat in the 19th century with the arrival of railways.

We have tried to encompass this guide to Winchester in five walks. Each one carries a different theme and if you do all of them you will come away with a fairly good picture of Winchester up to the 20th century. The walks vary from short and intense to long and wider-ranging. They can each be accomplished at a comfortable pace in about two hours. There are some hills to climb but this is largely unavoidable in Winchester.

We hope you enjoy the book, but most of all we hope you enjoy Winchester.

Bryan Dunleavy

Olena Thomas

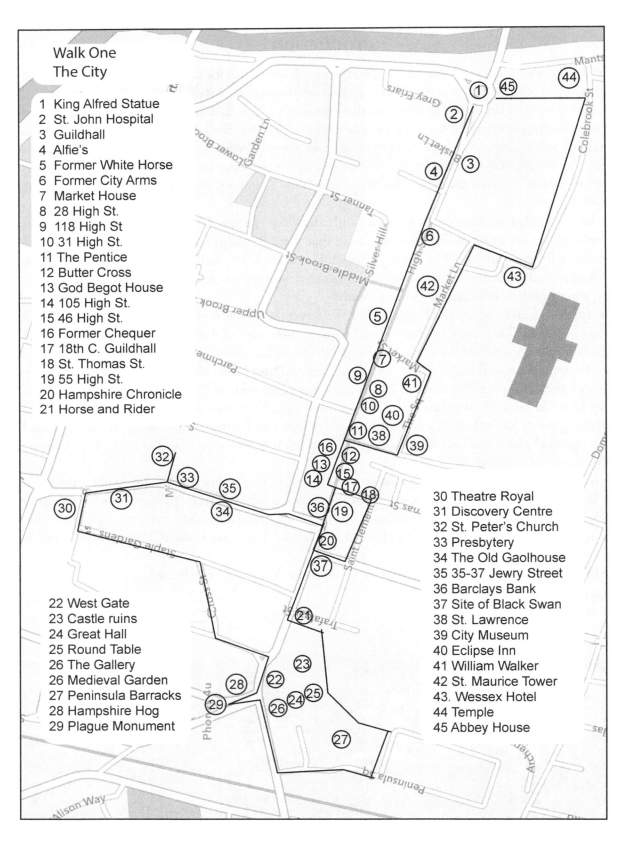

Walk One
The City

1 King Alfred Statue
2 St. John Hospital
3 Guildhall
4 Alfie's
5 Former White Horse
6 Former City Arms
7 Market House
8 28 High St.
9 118 High St
10 31 High St.
11 The Pentice
12 Butter Cross
13 God Begot House
14 105 High St.
15 46 High St.
16 Former Chequer
17 18th C. Guildhall
18 St. Thomas St.
19 55 High St.
20 Hampshire Chronicle
21 Horse and Rider

22 West Gate
23 Castle ruins
24 Great Hall
25 Round Table
26 The Gallery
26 Medieval Garden
27 Peninsula Barracks
28 Hampshire Hog
29 Plague Monument

30 Theatre Royal
31 Discovery Centre
32 St. Peter's Church
33 Presbytery
34 The Old Gaolhouse
35 35-37 Jewry Street
36 Barclays Bank
37 Site of Black Swan
38 St. Lawrence
39 City Museum
40 Eclipse Inn
41 William Walker
42 St. Maurice Tower
43. Wessex Hotel
44 Temple
45 Abbey House

Walk One: The City

Start by King Alfred's statue at the former East gate to the city. The walk will take you up the old Roman High Street. The High Street represents commercial and civic Winchester, all the way from the East Gate to the West Gate and there is a range of architectural styles on display, from a Norman arch, to medieval merchant houses, through examples from the 16th, 17th, 18th, 19th and 20th centuries.

Westgate marks the end of the High Street proper and the tower houses a small museum with an excellent view from the top platform.

Turn left here to explore "royal" Winchester. Most of these buildings have been County Council buildings for over a century, but before that, all the way back to 1067 when William I built a castle on this spot it was very much royal territory. Here are the ruins of some of the castle foundations, the 13th century Great Hall, the famous round table is displayed in the hall and there is a gallery off the hall displaying drawings of the former castle and palaces.

Walk through the Great Hall to the former Peninsula Barracks. These were built in 1796 on the site of the palace of Charles II. There are several military museums here.

Leave the barracks by the Romsey road and walk down towards Westgate. The High Street extension has a monument erected as a memorial to the plague of 1667.

Take Tower Street and work your way down to Jewry Street. On this corner is the Theatre Royal and the former Corn Exchange, now a Discovery Centre. Turn south along Jewry Street which has interesting buildings from the 18th to the 20th century.

Here you can rejoin the High Street and walk down to the Butter Cross. Cut through the passage to Great Minster Street. The final leg goes east along the Square, along Market Lane and Colebrook Street to the Abbey Gardens and the starting point of this walk.

King Alfred's Statue

The East Gate to the city used to stand here. It is now long gone, removed during a general demolition of the walls in 1791. City walls, so essential for protection in the Middle Ages, had become redundant well before the 18th century and had been left to fall into ruin. The eastern gateway was then opened by stages in the 19th century to become that part of the High Street known as Broadway.

The statue of King Alfred, erected at the very end of the 19th century, commands Winchester's High Street, which was laid down 2000 years ago. This was the commercial street, the "Cheap" (shopping) Street of the town, while either side of the statue religious foundations occupied the land in medieval times.

On Alfred's left was the monastery of St. Mary, known as Nunnaminster. On the right stood the house of the Dominican Friars and St John's Hospital.

King Alfred's (1) bronze statue now commands the entrance to Winchester. He is probably the most famous of the west Saxon kings and is credited with setting Wessex on a course to dominance and eventual absorption of all the kingdoms of England into a single country.

The statue, dates from Victorian times and was designed by Hamo Thorneycroft, a member of the Royal Academy. It is a bronze casting 17 feet high from foot to raised arm. The sword was apparently made separately from the casting. The bronze was mounted on block of Cornish granite and that in turn was mounted on another rough hewn block. The depiction of Alfred probably owes more to the Victorian conception of a Saxon warrior than the reality. Contemporary portrayals of Alfred, on the face of coins and on the Ashmolean jewel, show him to be clean shaven rather than with a long flowing beard. And while he is rightly created with turning the tide against the Danish invasions, his legacy owes more to his status as a law giver and concern for the cultural elevation of the nation.

The dedication of the statue was a big event in Winchester in September 1899, 1000 years after Alfred's death. Every dignitary, including the Bishop of Winchester was present and crowds lined the streets to watch parades to mark the occasion. The statue itself was finally complete and installed two years later when it was erected on its plinth.

Alfred himself was originally buried in the Minster of St Swithun, now Winchester Cathedral, but it was Alfred's intention and his will that a new Minster be built, as indeed it was, just to the north of the old one. His son was entrusted with the foundation and construction began in 901. The new church was consecrated in 903 and Alfred's remains were carried with due ceremony from the first resting place. The two monasteries lived side by side in less than easy harmony until 1109, when the monks of the new minster acquired land north of the city walls in

Opposite: *St. John's Hospital as seen from Broadway and below: the almshouses at the back.*

Hyde Meadow. They decamped soon after this and built a new monastery. Alfred and other royal bodies travelled with them.

Unfortunately Hyde Abbey was one of those which was quickly dismantled after it was acquired by the crown in 1538. The new owner, Sir Thomas Wriothesley (later earl of Southampton) was only interested in the abbey's manors and quickly took the abbey buildings apart and sold the salvage. It is believed that the grave was not disturbed at the time.

This situation changed in 1788 when the site was acquired by the county magistrates to build a new prison. Many of the graves were disturbed as workmen cleared the site and the bones scattered.

Nevertheless there was some optimism that a part at least of Alfred's remains may have survived. A dig in 1999 under the place believed to be the site of the high altar of the abbey yielded a collection of bones. These were stored in a box at the City Museum for future examination.

Last year (2013) a grave at St Bartholemew's church was exhumed in great anticipation of discovering the remains of Alfred. Two skeletons were discovered but they later turned out to be of 13th century origin and neither one could possibly be Alfred. One of the archaeologists then turned to the cardboard box in the Winchester City Museum and early indications suggest that the dating of the pelvic bone (late 9th century to early 10th century) could either belong to Alfred or his son Edward.

Alfred remains the best known of all the English kings and is the only one to be given the appellation 'the great" The monument you see here marked the 1000th anniversary of his death.

The Hospital of St. John the Baptist

Across the Broadway is **St John's Hospital (2),** founded in 1275. Very little of it today can be distinguished from the 13th century original as it was largely rebuilt in the 18th century. For example, it has the rather curious feature of a false upper row of windows painted on the front

wall. The purpose of the hospital, founded by a wealthy alderman, John Devenyshe, was to provide overnight food and lodging for poor pilgrims and travellers. Winchester was a magnet in the middle ages and people would often arrive with few resources but a great deal of hope. The city fathers continued to support the foundation as it addressed a vagrancy problem in a practical way. The institution was dissolved by the government in 1546 but almost immediately re-granted to the city corporation.

The building largely held to its original function during the 15th and 16th centuries but the hall was often used for town meetings. The chapel was used in the 18th century as a school for poor children. In 1829, after some years of neglect, the corporation surrendered the hospital to an independent charitable foundation which restored its original purpose and built alms houses to the rear of the building. They can be seen through the gateway. On the opposite (south) side of the Broadway is an extension to the hospital built in the 19th century. The buildings behind this gatehouse are mostly of 20th century foundation.

The Guildhall

Over the centuries Winchester lost its primacy to London and slowly experienced economic decline. Estimates of population from the Domesday survey of 1086 project a population of 6,000 for Winchester, at that time second only to London in size. The Mint was maintained in the city untll at least the 13th century when coins were still minted with the head of Henry III and the treasury was also secured in Winchester in Norman times. By 1377, the year of the Poll Tax, the population was only 1440 and if we take into account the severe loss of population after 1349 this would mean that by the middle of the 14th century Winchester had already shrunk to 2,400 people. It's status as a city in terms of size in England had dwindled from second to thirtieth. The relative decline continued.

Winchester's 19th century Guildhall

18th Century Winchester could be described as a backwater. The ancient medieval capital had lost its importance and bishops of Winchester were no longer a force in the land. It is estimated that the population was about 4000 in the first part of the 18th century and under 6000 in 1801.

In 1724 Daniel Defoe wrote that Winchester was a 'place of no trade, no manufacture, no

navigation'. On the other hand 'here is a great deal of good company the abundance of gentry being in the neighbourhood, it adds to the sociableness of the place. The clergy here are generally speaking very rich and numerous'. In 1755 Horace Walpole called Winchester 'a paltry town and small'.

The arrival of the railway in 1840 transformed Winchester's prospects and this new prosperity was symbolised by a grand new **Guildhall (3)**. Most of the grounds of the old abbey were claimed for the project and buildings were cleared. The replacement impressively commands the lower High street today and is now one of Winchester's two most prominent buildings with its central gothic tower. The foundation stone was laid in 1871 and the new building was opened two years later. The building was extended in 1893.

Built into the north wall are some publicly visible weather instruments showing temperature and barometric pressure. Many years before the ages of radio and television weather forecasts and iphone apps instruments like these performed a public information service. The tourist information office is located at street level.

Some of the oldest medieval buildings on the High Street. Although much modified over the centuries, the range from 31 to 35 still have timbers which can be dated to 1340.

On this page: 31 High Street

On page 11: aspectsof 33-35 Hgh Street.

If you have time the Guildhall often has exhibitions in the spacious public areas.

The High Street

The High Street, which rises sharply from Broadway to the West Gate was once part of the east-west road from Farnham, where the bishop had a palace to the next bishop's see at Salisbury. The town is in a valley and the High Street, laid out in Roman times, rises steadily upwards to the West Gate. In Saxon times it acquired the name of Cheap Street, that is the market or shopping street. Over time the word *cheap* became associated with bargain and latterly came to mean inexpensive and of low quality, but it was not always so. A Cheap Street survives today in London unchanged and the word prevails in the market town of Chipping Norton in Oxfordshire. The name was changed in the 18th century for the grander sounding High Street, however, its function as Winchester's main commercial street is unchanged.

It is easy to imagine the congestion that would occur if today's flume of traffic was still routed through the town. Indeed a by-pass came quite early to Winchester when the Southampton to Basingstoke road circumvented the town in 1940. Even so, traffic still had access to the High Street until comparatively recent times. Accordingly there were many inns along this street, at one time as many as 23. Not much of this history is recognisable today.

Only in the lower High Street on Broadway is an 18th or 19th century inn, now called **Alfies (4),** with an arched entrance to the courtyard, is there a nod to the days of the coaching trade. Further up, a three story flint and brick building, much remodelled of course into shop units, which acknowledges its past by retaining or incorporating the former name. The former **White Horse Inn (5)** has its name embedded in the flint. 200 years ago the High Street had signs such as the Bakers Arms. Bell & Crown, Black Swan, City Arms, Coach & Horses, Crown & Anchor, Dolphin, George, Globe, India Arms, Marquis of Granby, Plume of Feathers, Railway Tavern, Royal Oak, Star, Vine, White Hart, and White Horse.

The City Arms was at **7-8 High street. (6)** It was the Queen's Head until 1802, when it

Above: A view of the High Street from the Butter Cross

Below: The 15th Century God Begot House. (13)

acquired the new name. The present building replaced the former inn in 1873 and became a Co-op store. The Globe was also in this area but was one of the buildings demolished to make way for the new Guildhall.

From Market Street the road narrows. At ground level these are all, mostly modern shop frontages and so you will not learn much about the origin of these buildings from ground level. You must look upwards. There is quite a useful book published a few years ago entitled *Look Up Winchester* which portrays many of these buildings through their upper floor architecture through excellent photographs in true perspective and knowledgeable descriptions. You may find a copy in one of Winchester's bookshops.

From here you should take the trouble to look up to the second and third stories and see clues about the origin of the buildings. This street has been here a very long time and below ground there will be foundations that go back 1000 years. Above ground the structures have invariably been rebuilt or modified. Parts have been retained and others adapted, with additions here and there. The overall impression is a charming higgledy piggledy collection. It would no doubt be a town planner's nightmare, but for the tourist and residents who use Winchester's shops it is a pleasure to see a town grow organically.

Street numbering adopts the simple expedient of numbering consecutively on one side up to the West Gate and returning down the street on the other side. As we go up the street we can look at some of the more interesting buildings on both sides.

There are several examples of 18th century bow windows in the upper stories - ingenious structures to capture as much daylight as possible. Several shop frontages from the early 20th century have been retained.

At the corner of Market Street is the former **Market House. (7)** It was built in 1857 and draws attention to itself because of its doric

columns. It was principally a vegetable market but has since been converted to other uses. The house at **Number 28 (8)** has double upper bow windows, of which there are many examples to be found in Winchester's older streets. On the other side, the building at **118 (9),** was formerly a chapel. It is now occupied by the *Body Shop* but above the shop front is a large central window which may give a clue to its original institutional purpose. The walls have pilasters up each side and a pediment above.

The High Street narrows further at **Number 29 (10),** where a longish colonnade supports jetties overhanging the ground level. This section is known as the *Pentice* and contains a mixture of buildings ranging back almost seven centuries. The timbers have been scientifically dated in recent years and one of them has roof timbers cut down between 1339 and 1340. This particular one is **Number 35 High Street (11),** an extension

of Boots the Chemist. Parts of this building are therefore well into its seventh century. The other gables in this group, numbers 33 and 34 have been given a date of 1459 - 1464.

Number 32 is a Victorian rebuild and Number 31, presently Starbucks, also appears to be late medieval. The main Boots shop, overpowering the others at three stories high is a completely modern building, engineered with precisely cut timbers and leaded lights, to look like a late Tudor building. It is of course nothing of the kind.

At the western corner of the Pentice the street opens up to a small piazza. Here is the stone cross, known locally as the **Butter Cross. (12)** The cross itself was principally a designated meeting place first built between 1422 and 1461.

The Butter Cross
On page 15:The closk on the former Guildhall

14

It was restored and added to in 1865 to a design by the architect Sir Gilbert Scott, so although it looks medieval, the upper part is largely of Victorian design. It is said that the two buildings crowded behind it were two alehouses in medieval times popularly known as *Hevyn and Helle*. They were once separated by a passage that led to St Lawrence's church immediately behind, but this has since been filled in. *Hevyn* was replaced by the 14th century gabled building which still stands and was known as *Le Newe Place*. This building, squeezed behind the butter cross, is probably the oldest 14th century building on the street. It is three stories high and backs onto the church. Timbers within the building have been dated between 1316 and 1352 and there are some stone foundation walls associated with the old Norman palace. Today it is an eating house so you can go inside, duck your head as you mind the beams and experience the floors which have not been flat and even for many, many years.

The building next to it on the other side of the passage has a rather ugly 18th century frontage which conceals its earlier date. The timbers here have been dated to 1508. and there is a Tudor fireplace inside. As with the companion building across the passage this also includes some remains of the Norman palace wall.

Across the street on the north side is another prominent medieval building, known as **"God Begot" house.(13)** It has nothing to do with God, although it was at one time a cathedral property. The name comes from the Saxon *"god begeaton"* meaning "good bargain" indicating that the properties there could be had for a low rental. The present structure dates to 1462 and was part of a square of tenements, much of which has since been rebuilt.

There are also some impressive 18th century buildings in this part of the High Street. **Number 105 (14)** for example, now occupied by the National Westminster bank, was, at one time a very grand town house indeed. On the south side,

Number 46 (15), displays a huge arched window, part of some remodelling in undertaken in 1806 for the White Hart Inn. The window provided a platform for the Duke of Wellington to address a crowd during an election campaign. The inn closed in 1857 due to the decline in the coaching trade and the ground floor was converted into shops. One imagines that this impressive window lit the room over the entrance way to the inn yard when it was first built.

Opposite, although the 19th century frontage would not betray this, stood one of the great medieval inns of Winchester, the **Chequer. (16)** The proprietor, James Dibsdale, removed himself to the George Inn on the corner of Jewry Street sometime before 1780. The Chequer was demolished and the present building replaced it. The upper stories have elegant bow windows. The ground floor, divided for mixed retail use, has stylish arched windows which are probably early 20th century.

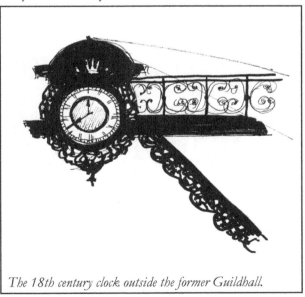

The 18th century clock outside the former Guildhall.

Although I have remarked earlier that Winchester was in decline in the 18th century, there was some optimism among the merchants in Winchester because in 1711 they built a new guildhall on the site of the old one which had been erected in 1361. It is now **Lloyds Bank**

This building (15) was formerly The White Hart Inn.

(17) and a new frontage faces the building. It can be recognised by two prominent features, the massive clock which overhangs the street and the statue of Queen Anne. Both were donated by prominent Winchester figures, the clock by Sir William Paulet and the statue by George Bridges then MP for Winchester.

The back of the building, which can be seen from **St Thomas Street (18)** may give a better idea of the origins of the 300 year old building with its wall covered by pan tiles. You can also get a better view of the small belfry on top of the building.

The western corner used to be home to The Dolphin, one of Winchester's medieval inns. Its replacement was designed and built in 1882 as a home for Richard Moss, brewer and M.P. The land was owned by St John's Hospital.

A rather striking faux-Tudor building at **Number 56 (19),** presently a men's clothing store, dates only from 1912 when two properties were demolished to build Winchester's first cinema, *The Picture House.*

55-6 High Street, Winchester's First Cinema in 1912

The corner of the High Street and St Thomas Street

Next door at **Number 57 (20)** a double fronted bow window dating from the 18ᵗʰ century. Until recently this was the home to the Hampshire Chronicle but is now a restaurant. The hand

The West Gate

Above: a view down the High Street

painted inscription above the window "Jacob and Johnson" has been retained. The newspaper had been printed at this location since 1807. In 1991 the printing was moved to a modern plant although the newspaper kept its office here until 2004. Jacob and Johnson became the publishers in the 19th century.

The upper part of the High Street has been largely redeveloped in the 20th century but some 18th century buildings remain. The corner of Southgate Street was once the site of the Black Swan, a substantial 19th century inn which has some residual fame as the fictional Sherlock Holmes once stayed there. Now it is entirely modern residential and retail development.

Elizabeth Frink

Beside the street, sheltered by trees, a very fine bronze of a **horse and rider (21)** by Elisabeth Frink. She was one of England's finer sculptors. She was born in Suffolk in 1930 and achieved world renown as a sculptor before her death in 1993. The naked man on a horse was cast in 1975. Horses were one of the themes she explored and this is a good example.

The West Gate stands as a reminder of the time when Winchester was a walled city. Walls and gates were originally defensive and later used to control traffic or charge tolls. Eventually they lost their purpose and were neglected and in 1791 most of Winchester's walls and gates were pulled down. The **Westgate (22)** is the sole survivor of the principal entrances to the city, and it was still the western entrance to the town in the age of the motor car. Buildings were taken down during redevelopment to create a road going round the tower. The foundation is Saxon but this version of it was rebuilt in the 13th century and modified with a cannon platform in the 14th. Until the High Street was pedestrianised this was the western entrance to the street for traffic and an old inn, the *Plume of Feathers* abutted the walls on the north side.

The old north, east and south gates were demolished in the 18th century. Northgate collapsed in 1755 while a christening party was using the building. There are no reports of injury, although this is not to say there were none. It was subsequently pulled down. In 1771 Winchester established a paving commission to provide footpaths and better roads and during their work in the last part of the 18th century South Gate, on what was then called Gold Street was demolished, together with the East Gate.

The West Gate was used as a debtors prison from the 17th to the 19th century and this probably accounts for it being kept in good repair. The floor above the gate is now used as a museum and you can climb to the top of the tower for a good view down the High Street.

Here, turn left into the precinct that is largely given over to local government. The whole

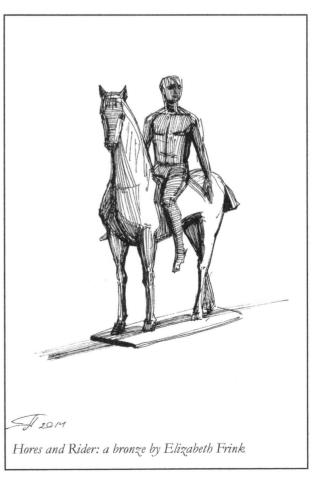

Hores and Rider: a bronze by Elizabeth Frink

Above: The interior of the 13th century Great Hall.

Below: 19th Century Hampshire County Council buildings.

area on both sides of the street is now packed with blocks attending to one facet or other of Hampshire's administration.

The south side of the High Street divides between what we might call ecclesiastical Winchester and Royal Winchester. There was once a Royal palace further down, almost on the edge of the Minster boundary but soon after gaining control of England in 1067 William set about building a **castle (23)** higher up the hill. This was not the only castle he built at this time - the most famous being the Tower of London. The castle retained its function until the 17th century civil war and it was a stronghold for the Royalists until it fell to Cromwell's forces in 1646. He immediately ordered the destruction of the castle. As a consequence nothing remains above ground today but some of the underground parts of the castle have been excavated, which you can see in this precinct.

The Great Hall

One building is medieval, the **Great Hall (24)** of Henry III, built between 1222 and 1235. It became County Hall in the 18th century. and there are some Victorian additions which integrate quite well. Unfortunately the brutalist design of the Law Courts rather spoils things but Winchester doesn't get everything right.

The Great Hall, is an impressive royal hall which can only be surpassed by Westminster Hall in London. The famous **Round Table (25)** is on display at one end of the hall.

The Round Table has legendary fame and is associated with the real or mythical king Arthur. It makes its first documentary appearance in the middle of the 12th century but the idea of a group of equals, symbolised by the round table, was potent in the middle ages and the idea gained traction during the "Age of Chivalry" when stories were collected about King Arthur and his knights. The later Plantagenet and Tudor kings were interested in the legend and the concept of the "once and future king."

This table has been subjected to scientific testing and dated to the years 1250-1280 and it has been suggested by one scholar that the table was made for a tournament near Winchester on 20th April 1290, during the reign of Edward I.

The paintwork dates from the Tudor age. Henry VIII had an older brother who was named Arthur with the deliberate intention of connecting the legendary king with the new Tudor dynasty. Prince Arthur died at the age of 16 and the succession passed to his younger brother Henry.

It is worth going through the Great Hall into **The Gallery (26)** within the Victorian administrative buildings. Here you can learn about the royal afterlife of the castle and see some drawings of the ambitious plans for a palace to rival that of Versailles.

On the steep slopes from the old castle to the cathedral Charles II planned a terrace of ornamental gardens with a central mall leading down to the Cathedral West entrance. In fact he went so far in 1683 to issue an order forbidding the Dean from selling any cathedral land and property that was within the purview of his plans. At the top of the hill the old castle was to be replaced by a magnificent 17th century palace. Had those plans gone ahead we might be marvelling today at this royal palace of Winchester.

Christopher Wren was commissioned to design the palace and building went ahead in 1683. Apparently the structure was completed

Buildings from the Peninsula Barracks, 1796

central fountain and ornamental gardens.

The barracks were built in 1796 and were occupied for almost 200 years. In 1986 the barracks were converted into private residential apartments with some of the buildings being retained for military museums. Those interested in military history can find much of interest in the *Gurkha Museum, The Rifles Display,* the *Museum of the King's Royal Hussars,* the *Greenjackets Museum, the Guardroom Museum* and the *Hampshire Regimental Museum* in **Serle's House (127)** on Southgate Street.

Head west towards the Romsey Road. The gatehouse is part museum and part coffee shop - a good stop for refreshment. Turn right down the road. Above the West Gate a circle opens up to take traffic to Romsey or Andover. More council offices have been built around this circle. A small bronze sculpture at ground level, which can be missed, is the **Hampshire Hog (28)**, by David Kemp.

At this junction is **monument (29)** erected in 1759 by a curiously named organisation called the Society of Natives. They were formed, according to the inscription n 26th August 1669 to provide for the widows and orphans of men who had lost their lives during the great plague of 1666, apparently reaching Winchester a year after London.

but it was never finished. Charles died two years later and after his death there was neither sufficient will nor funds to complete the work. There it seems to have languished.In 1796 it was incorporated into the Peninsula barracks complex and some of the masonry was reused in the new project. However, a fire gutted this building in 1894 and the subsequent rebuild has only preserved the pediment.

Make your way now through the Great Hall to the reconstructed **medieval garden (26).** There are some step to take you to the Peninsula Barracks and the former parade ground.

The **Peninsula Barracks (27)** are as fine a set of buildings as could grace any city. The buildings in red brick with stone porticos and embellishments laid out in spacious square are certainly pleasing to the eye. The former parade ground has been re-designed as a square with a

The Plague Monument

On facing page: The West Gate and above, the view from the top platform down the High Street.

From the West Gate go north along Tower Street, bear right along Cross Street to Staple Gardens. Continue north for a short walk and come out on Jewry Street just beside the **Theatre Royal (30).**

The Theatre Royal is a name often associated with 18th century theatres but this one is relatively young as a theatre. It first opened in 1850 as The Market Hotel. As it was next door to the Corn Exchange it was a convenient location for farmers coming into town on business. The hotel was converted to entertainment in 1914, showing music hall variety acts and short silent films and newsreels. In 1920 it became a full time cinema and lasted in this form until 1974 when there was a general decline in the popularity of cinema entertainment. At this time the building faced the prospect of demolition but it was rescued by joint action from Winchester City Council and public subscription and the building was saved for the presentation of live theatre.

It has been a success story. Public support and grants of funding have enabled the theatre to purchase neighbouring buildings and undertake refurbishment programs. At the time of writing the Theatre Royal as a house of entertainment has reached its centenary.

There was once an 18th century purpose built theatre on the opposite side of Jewry Street, now occupied by 20th century buildings. This theatre opened in 1785 and went out of business in 1861.

The rather interesting Italianate building next door opened in 1838 as a **Corn Exchange (31).** Yellow brick appears to have been popular at this period in Winchester and there are many buildings dotted around the town using brick of this colour. Here the rather dirty character this brick can sometimes acquire with age has been appealingly balanced by the use of white stone. For many years the building functioned as a public library but it has recently been adapted into a multi-purpose building for arts and learning

Two impressive buildings on Jewry Street from the 19th Century.

Top: The Discovery Centre

Below: The Old Gaol House

called *The Discovery Centre*.

More-or-less opposite is the Roman Catholic Church of **St Peter (32)**. The present structure is less than 100 years old although the style would suggest something much older. One interesting feature embedded in the north wall and clearly of a different age entirely, is a 12th century arch surrounding a doorway. This was salvaged from the old St Mary Magdalen Hospital to the east of Winchester. This hospital was a medieval foundation as a leper colony and like such hospitals was placed well beyond the bounds of the city for fear that leprosy was contagious. It survived the Reformation but was commandeered by the government in 1665 to accommodate Dutch prisoners of war. Much of the carved woodwork and panelling was used for firewood during these years and the institution never quite recovered. It limped along until 1788 when it was demolished and the materials were reused to build six almshouses on Water Lane. The salvaged door is now the only identifiable remnant.

Next to the church is an impressive Georgian building which functions as a **presbytery (33)**.

More yellow brick, although of a decidedly grey cast, is to be found above the J. D. Wetherspoon pub **"The Old Gaolhouse." (34)** The name is not a flight of fancy, because this was indeed the original purpose of the building. It was built in 1805. However, this is not the whole story, because the block on the other side of the Church was also part of the gaol. This is presently a furniture shop. The church was sandwiched between the two blocks in the middle of the 19th century and also uses yellow brick.

Across the street is an early **19th century house (35)**, rendered and painted pale blue at the time of writing, with ten tapered stone columns at the front, formerly a shop for H. W. Frampton.

The block between St George's Street and the High Street, now dominated by the Georgian style **Barclays Bank (36)** building was once occupied by the George Inn, perhaps Winchester's premier inn, until it was demolished in 1956.

Take a short walk down to the Butter Cross. Go through the passage to Minster Street which opens up anther small square.

St Lawrence's Church (38), a small church boxed in by surrounding buildings, is not as old as one might expect. Pevsner thought it was 15th century however since his visit in the 1960s a 13th century doorway has been discovered on the north side, which is evidence of an earlier foundation. The doorway may have connected the church to the High Street before it was blocked off by the addition to the house at 42 High Street. This area was once the site of the Saxon Royal palace and it was not until the castle was developed that other buildings sprang up here.

The 12th century doorway in St. Peter's Church

Above: Barclay's Bank, which replaced the George Hotel in 1960.

Bottom: Winchester's City Museum

East window in St Lawrence Church

St Lawrence's Church from the High Street

On the right before the cathedral precinct is the **Winchester City Museum (39),** built for the purpose in 1891 with galleries on three floors. The ground floor displays shops and showcases from Winchester's more recent 19th and 20th century past. The middle floor displays artefacts from Saxon and Medieval periods, together with four models showing Winchester's development from Roman times to the late middle ages. The top floor displays Roman artefacts. Admission is free.

On the Market Square you will see a 16th century timber frame house that was once the rectory for the church. It is now a public house called the **Eclipse Inn (40)**.

The Square is a wide, comfortable street lined with shops in mostly late Victorian or early 20th century buildings. On the corner, the pub is called the **William Walker (41)** after the diver who worked at underpinning the cathedral with concrete early in the 20th century.

The building that fills Market Lane on the left was a Winchester municipal building which has now been converted to residences. In a gap on the left is a church tower, all that remains of the Church of **St Maurice (42)**. The church at one time dominated this section of the High Street and extended back to the lane with the yard gong back to the Cathedral Close. The church was apparently much enlarged and remodelled in 1842. All that survives today is the Norman archway preserved in the tower. The church was demolished in the late 1950s.

On the right is the **Wessex Hotel (43),** built in the early 1960s. Nicholas Pevsner, the distinguished architectural historian who visited Winchester in the 1960s, approved. He wrote in his survey of Hampshire's buildings, "This really is a triumph." One has to agree. Although it is a building in a modern idiom it sits comfortably

Abbey Gardens

The tower of the church of St. Maurice is all that remains of a very large church which filled this part of Winchester until the 20th century.

alongside the cathedral and the agglomeration of older buildings in Winchester. It is worth stepping inside the lobby to see the stained glass window by the acclaimed English artist John Piper.

The tour can now be completed by following Colebrook Street to the river. The **Temple (44)** building dates from 1751 when William Pescod built the **Abbey House (45)**. Apparently this was intended to hide the working mill from the view of the house. There were two other wings to this structure which have not survived.

The Abbey Gardens on the south side of Broadway are all that remains of another of Winchester's great religious foundations. This was the nunnery of St Mary, founded in the late 9th century by King Alfred and his Queen, Ealswith. It was popularly known as "Nunnaminster". The abbey was once bounded by the High Street and Colebrook Street and included a gatehouse, a Church, a great house for the abbess, a cloister, refectory, dormitory, as well as all the functional buildings - kitchen, buttery, brewery, bakehouse, granary, stables, and also a "plumber's" house, and of course a water mill. Much was swept away immediately after the dissolution but there were still some ruins in the early 17th century.

The present building on the grounds was built by William Pescod, Winchester's recorder (judge), around 1700. By a curious irony, when the French got round to closing their monasteries in 1790 a group of nuns crossed the channel and settled here in the building you can see, and for a period this part of Winchester once again had a nunnery. This building is now used as an official residence for the Mayor of Winchester.

You are now back at the starting point.

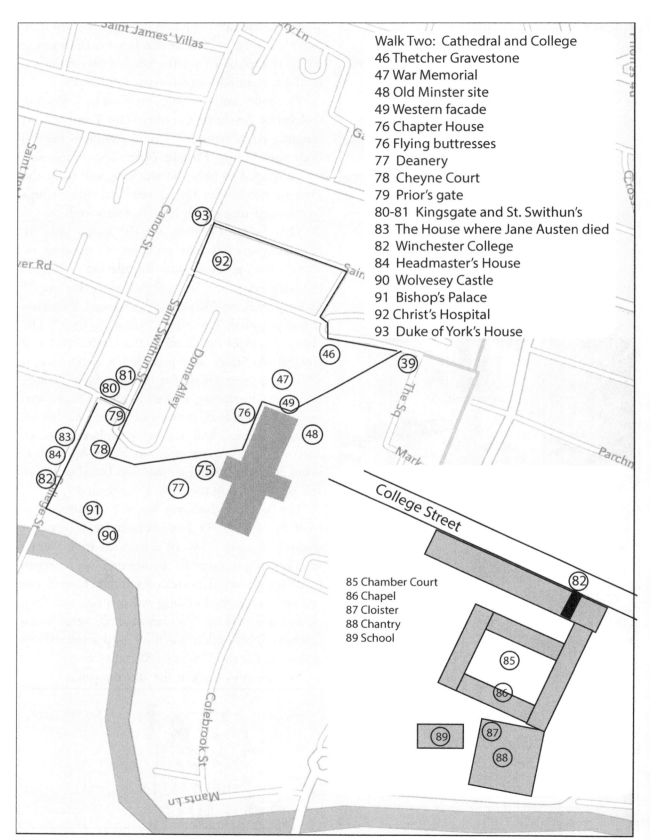

Walk Two: Cathedral and College
46 Thetcher Gravestone
47 War Memorial
48 Old Minster site
49 Western facade
76 Chapter House
76 Flying buttresses
77 Deanery
78 Cheyne Court
79 Prior's gate
80-81 Kingsgate and St. Swithun's
83 The House where Jane Austen died
82 Winchester College
84 Headmaster's House
90 Wolvesey Castle
91 Bishop's Palace
92 Christ's Hospital
93 Duke of York's House

College Street

85 Chamber Court
86 Chapel
87 Cloister
88 Chantry
89 School

Walk Two:
Ecclesiastical Winchester

The second walk around ecclesiastical Winchester is short in distance but densely packed with interesting things to see. It will probably take two hours at a minimum. The walk will explore the Cathedral and its precincts, Winchester College and, if you have time, Wolvesey Castle.

Wolvesey Castle can be taken with Walk 5 if you prefer.

The Cathedral Close is now largely open space with pathways. There are few monuments but one curiosity is the gravestone of one **Thomas Thetcher (46).** His story has so captured the imagination that the stone with its inscription has been replaced three times, in 1781, 1802 and 1996. The inscription now reads:

In Memory of

Thomas Thetcher a Grenadier in the North Reg. of Hants Militia, who died of a violent Fever contracted by drinking Small Beer when hot the 12 May 1764. Aged 26 Years.

In grateful remembrance of whose universal good will towards his Comrades, this Stone is placed here at their expence, as a small testimony of their regard and concern.

Here sleeps in peace a Hampshire Grenadier,
Who caught his death by drinking cold small Beer,
Soldiers be wise from his untimely fall
And when ye're hot drink Strong or none at all.
This memorial being decay'd was restor'd by the Officers of the Garrison A.D. 1781.
An Honest Soldier never is forgot
Whether he die by Musket or by Pot.
The Stone was replaced by the North Hants Militia when disembodied at Winchester, on 26 April 1802, in consequence of the original Stone being destroyed.
And again replaced by The Royal Hampshire Regiment 1966.

The inscription has sometimes been wrongly interpreted as drinking hot beer, rather than drinking when hot. The moral expressed here is that "when ye're hot drink Stong or none at all." Small beer had a very low alcoholic content, and in the days when water supplies could not be guaranteed pure was, in effect, a water substitute. Usually the process of making the ale, boiling the water and fermentation would be enough to kill any harmful microbes that might be in the water. In this case the unlucky and thirsty Trooper Thetcher quickly downed quantities of weak ale that had not been properly made. Sadly, this killed him.

War Memorial at the west of the Cathedral

The west facade of the Cathedral. originally had two towers and extended a further 40 feet to the west. The towers were becoming unsafe in the 14th century and the present frontage was built under the direction of Bishop William Edington according to the style of the period.

The other memorial of note is the bronze statue of a World War I soldier (47) on a plinth outside the west entrance to the cathedral. The memorial stands to the memory of soldiers of the King's Royal Rifle Corps who gave their lives in the 1914-18 war and in the second war of 1939-45. It was designed by John Tweed and erected in 1922.

To the north of the cathedral you can see the excavation outlines of the former minster (48), together with illustration boards. Although the present cathedral has been there for over 1000 years it is by no means the first building on the site. Excavations were undertaken in the 1960s and 1970s and the information boards explain the somewhat confusing history of the early buildings on this site. The first minster may have a history reaching as far back as 635, but little is known of this building. It was enlarged in the 9th century and substantially rebuilt after 971 during the time of Bishop Ethelwold. This was the building you can see in outline on the ground. It was demolished in 1093 in favour of the completed Norman minster, the Saxon building was barely over its first century.

To complicate matters further, a new minster was founded in 903 by the side of the "old" minster and this state of affairs continued until the New Minster removed themselves to Hyde in 1110. The history of this abbey will be discussed in Walk 3.

The present cathedral was originally the monastery church. After the Reformation it became the cathedral church of the bishop and the prior of the monastery was translated to the dean of the cathedral. This building's foundation dates to 1079 when the new Norman bishop, Wakelin, started construction.

The western facade (49) was built by Bishop William Edington in the 14th century. The original building had twin towers, but they were deemed unsafe and a rebuild was ordered. During this reconstruction the west end was shortened

Windows on the north side

by about 40 feet.

Even so, the cathedral is the longest in the country at 534 feet but at its cross stands a low squat tower. It looks unfinished. One might conclude that either a planned tower or spire was not completed, or one was built and it fell down. That is in fact what happened. The year was 1107, only a few years after the new minster was completed.

The tower, which was said to rise five stories above the roof of the nave, was finished in 1100, the year of King William II's death in a hunting accident in the New Forest. William was buried there a few days later, not, it should be added, with much enthusiasm by the monks who disapproved of their former king's morality. Seven years later the tower collapsed, almost certainly due to inadequate foundations, but it did not take the medieval mind long to connect this collapse with the burial of William and see God's judgement upon him.

Despite this misadventure the cathedral has survived, although that in itself is remarkable because Winchester Cathedral, a little like Venice, is built on uncertain foundations. When Bishop Wakelin set out to build the minster he got permission from William the Conqueror to cut down all the timber he could within four days from Hampage Wood, a few miles to the east of Winchester. William did not imagine that much would be taken but the bishop had other ideas and organised a large gang of men to cut down the wood day and night for the permitted time and practically obliterated the wood in the process. Why so much wood was needed only became clear in the 20th century when it was apparent that parts of the cathedral were sinking and the structure was seriously in danger of collapse. The walls needed underpinning. The engineers dug down eight feet to discover that the whole building was built on a raft of logs, by this time, after 800 years, a peat bog. Wakelin's prime need for so much timber was not for construction of scaffolding, roofs and partitions but for the very foundation of the cathedral. The building was rescued in the 20th century by concrete underpinnings and the diver, William Walker, who put the concrete in place, became quite famous in these parts and has a pub on **Market Street (42)** named after him.

Saint Swithun

If you are ever in Winchester on a rainy day, spare a thought for Saint Swithun. There is a legend that if it rains on St Swithuns day July 15th, then you are doomed to forty more consecutive days of rain. If however the sun is shining your luck is in and you have a summer ahead of you.

Swithun was actually a real man and probably a great one. He was Bishop of Winchester until his death in 862 and he was certainly much venerated after his death.

About his life we know little other than he was bishop for the last ten years of his life. It is during the afterlife of Swithun that the legend grows.

100 years after his death Dunstan decided to make him the patron of the new Winchester minster and accordingly his body was removed to the new basilica. Miracles were reported. And St Swithun's shrine became a much visited place.

So what of the legend? Is there any truth in it? The drought part of it can be discounted because periods of drought of that length are entirely unknown in England. You are on more of a

Winchester Cathedral Plan

68 Richard Fox
69 Stephen Gardiner
70 Henry of Blois
71 St. Swithun
72 South Transept
73 Izaak Walton
74 Bishop Morley library

50 The Nave
51 Mezzanine
52 West Window
53 Jane Austen's Grave
54 Tournai Font
55 Choir
56 Tomb of King William II
57 North Transept
58 Epiphany Chapel
59 Holy Sepulchre Chapel
60 Crypt
61 Gaveston Tomb
62 Great Screen
63 Mortuary Chests
64 William of Edington
65 William of Wykeham
66 Cardinal Beaufort
67 William Waynflete

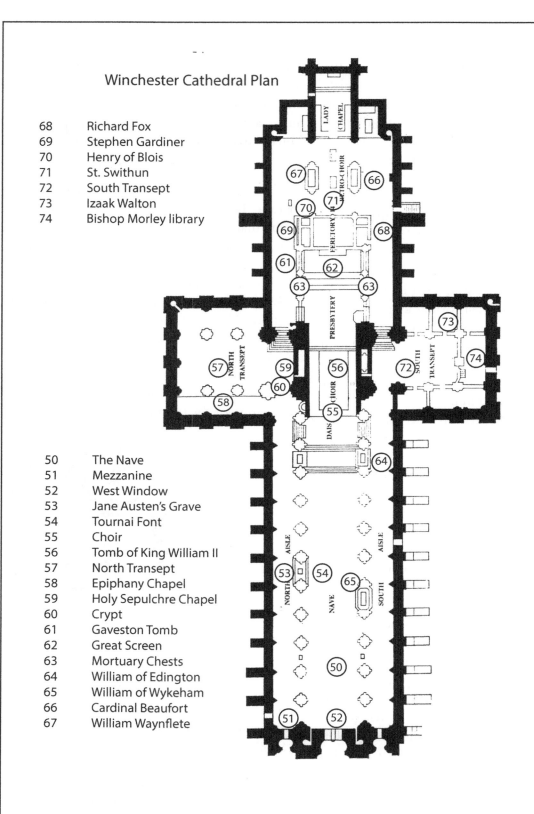

banker with rain, although even here a summer deluge would be unlikely.

That being said, there is some scientific basis for the legend. The jet stream often settles into a stable pattern around the middle of July. If is lies to the north of the UK in the summer then warm air will be drawn north from the Mediterranean and the Summer will be warm and dry. If on the other hand the jet stream settles to the south, colder and wetter systems will expected in England.

Be that as it may, the bones of St Swithun were much moved. The original resting place was in a modest grave outside the old minster and after a short period were moved inside the minster church. In 971, his remains were moved to a new tomb inside the new Minster, now the present cathedral. We don't know if that was a summer of torrential rain or whether it was a later year when rain fell on St. Swithun's day (July 15th) and continued for most of the summer. It was most likely in a later century because the legend does not emerge until the early 14th century. Over the years his tomb became a shrine and many miracles were attributed to the saint and a great many relics were acquired, each of course with certain attributable supernatural powers.

Swithun's bone were rudely disturbed one night during the reformation of the monasteries. The determination to end the life of all monasteries had been concluded and in the late 1530s these plans were put into effect. The transition from priory to cathedral was relatively smooth for Winchester, aided no doubt by the last Prior, a compliant William Kingsmill, who became the first Dean of the Cathedral. The general popularity of St. Swithun flagged a potential issue for the authorities as the demolition of the shrine might provoke demonstrations and even riots. The work was done in the dead of night.

Sir Thomas Wriothesley, Cromwell's agent for the takeover, and later Earl of Southampton, arranged for his team to arrive at 3 o'clock in the morning on September 21st 1538, and for the proceedings to be witnessed by the mayor and aldermen and senior members of the priory. Under their watchful eye they took inventory of all the treaure, items in gold, silver and bejewelled ornaments and cleaned out all of the 'idolatrous' relics - the vials of the blood of Christ, the splinters of the true cross, the bones and so on.

The given reason for this distinguished group of observers was to remove a temptation to idolatry but one suspects that the deeper reason was greed. The shrine was reputed to be a source of fabulous wealth. Wriothesley was disappointed. The jewel-encrusted *Cross of Jerusalem* turned out to be a fake; the jewels were coloured glass. Obviously someone had been there before him!

The story of St Swithun does not end there. In 1971 excavations around the old minster discovered Swithun's original grave and a stone donated by the church of St Swithun in Stavanger Norway (a church founded buy a disciple of Swithun) was laid there in commemoration.

The Cathedral District

Although Winchester is not very big by modern standards in medieval times it could be described as two towns: civic Winchester, which we largely covered in the first walk, and ecclesiastical Winchester, which we are to walk

Above: A view from the Mezzanine

Below: The Tournai Font

today. This whole area was once a large complex: a bishop's palace and castle, two monasteries, a nunnery, a college, and later a Carmelite friary. And beyond that, on the other side of the river the east soke, also part of the bishop's jurisdiction - the bishop's soke. Odd as it may appear to us now, the people living here were subject to different laws than those living in the town. This state of affairs lasted until 1835.

Let's start with the cathedral, Winchester's impressive monument to over 1000 years of history. This is the nerve centre of what might be called episcopal Winchester on land once owned and controlled by the bishops of Winchester.

The Cathedral Interior

What you see as you enter this impressive building has considerably changed from the original sponsored by Bishop Wakelin in 1067, although the bones of this building are still there. The original architecture, designed and built by Hugh the Mason, was in the Norman style with rounded arches, but two successive bishops in the 14th century, William of Edington and William of Wykeham, transformed the building. Edington, who had the seat from 1346 until his death twenty years later, focussed his attention on the west end.

William of Wykeham succeeded in 1366 and began a more ambitious program. William knew a thing or two about building and in his earlier progress through the ranks of government administration he had been a clerk of works during the development of Windsor castle as well as other royal buildings, and was able to find a talented builder (we would probably now call him an architect) William of Wyneford. Wyneford had already established a good reputation at Windsor, Abingdon and Wells and he entered into a partnership with Bishop Wykeham that would lead to both Winchester College and New College Oxford.

The Norman **Nave (50)** was supported by three tiers of rounded arches. Wyneford replaced these by two tiers of perpendicular arches to create the soaring effect of the nave today. To get some idea of what it looked like before the changes, take a look at the arches in the south transept. The pillars were strengthened to support the stone tracery of the arched roof.

Just inside the cathedral entrance is a **mezzanine (51)** where some of the cathedral plate is on display in glass cabinets.

Royal occasions

As one might expect the cathedral has been the site of some great royal occasions. William I set a precedent and a tradition by being crowned in Westmister Abbey in London in 1066, but there were two exceptions. Henry II's eldest son Henry was crowned here in 1172 although he never became a king with power. This requires some explanation. Henry II was still king of England but under pressure from his vigorous and ambitious sons he made some attempt to divide his empire. His eldest son was crowned here at Winchester with the understanding that he would inherit England, although Henry did not actually give him any power at the time. He was known as the "Young King." Richard was made Duke of Aquitaine, a vast territory in South-western France. Geoffrey was created Duke of Brittany and John, who was only six years-old at the time, got nothing. His father joked that he was John "Sans Terre", in English "Lackland", and the name stuck, even though John eventually, for a time at any rate, got it all. Henry the Young King died in 1183 before his father and never succeeded to the throne.

Richard I was also crowned here in 1194. This was his second coronation. During his ten year reign from 1189 to his death in 1199 he spent only a few months in England. His interests lay elsewhere. The second coronation was deemed advisable after his release from German captivity following his capture on the way back from the Crusade. By this time he had been absent from

The Great Screen

the kingdom for five years and since the English taxpayer had provided most of his ransom the show of a second coronation was a way of reinforcing his bond with the nation. He was probably on his way back to France at the time.

Winchester was also chosen for two royal weddings. Henry IV married Joan of Navarre here on February 7th 1403. She was his second wife.

The last royal wedding was that of the unfortunate Queen Mary to Phillip of Spain. She was married there by the conservative and pro-Roman Catholic bishop Stephen Gardiner and it was her efforts to turn back the clock that created her short, bloody and heir-less reign. Gardiner is depicted as a skeleton above his tomb, a gruesome reminder of the grim reaper. The Cathedral also preserves a chair covered in faded blue velvet. This is the chair Mary used during her marriage ceremony.

The Arthurian legend held the imagination in the middle ages and the Round Table, on display in the Great Hall, is undoubtedly an artefact from this period. Any connection with Arthur had great potency and Henry Tudor, feeling some pangs of insecurity on his newly won throne, deliberately named his first son Arthur. Had all gone to plan a King Arthur would have ascended the throne in 1509 but soon after his marriage to Katherine he died in 1502 in Ludlow of an illness and his younger brother Henry became his father's successor. Queen Elizabeth gave birth to Arthur, probably by design at Winchester as it was associated in the minds of some with Camelot, on September 22nd 1486. He was baptised in the Priory on the following Sunday. This was a major and splendid occasion.

The Window

The great stained glass **window (52)** in the western wall looks modern and abstract. It is not; most of the glass is medieval. After the parliamentary soldiers took Winchester in 1646 there was a lot of wanton destruction and the great window, offensive to the eyes of some puritans, was deliberately smashed. After matters calmed down the fragments of glass were gathered and the window was rebuilt in 1660, but as it was not possible to reconstruct the window as it once was, the glass was reassembled in a random manner. This is the result.

Some medieval wall paintings can be discovered in the **Holy Sepulchre chapel (59)**. They date from the 12th century and were only uncovered during the 1960s. They are in a remarkably good state of preservation and illustrate Christ being taken down from the cross and placed in his tomb.

North Aisle

Jane Austen (53) is rightly associated with Hampshire where she lived for most of her life, yet her memorial is in Winchester where she moved for the last two months of her life in a desperate attempt to seek a cure for the illness that was undermining her health. To this end she moved to a house in College Street, which is today marked by a plaque, where she was treated by a Mr. Lyford.

His efforts were of no avail and she died on July 18th 1817 at the early age of 41. Her illness was diagnosed in the 20th century as Addison's Disease, a condition which brought about the degradation of the adrenal glands. At that date, whatever optimism Mr. Lyford may have encouraged, there was no known cure.

By this time she was celebrated enough to warrant burial in the cathedral which was conducted with due ceremony on 24th July 1817. A brass plate marking her grave is in the northern aisle of the cathedral.

Almost opposite is the **Tournai font (54)** - a square, black stone, decorated around the sides with figures and resting on a pedestal. The stone, a black limestone which could be polished, came from Tournai in Belgium and appears to have been much favoured for fonts as there are several in the country.

The Choir

The choir is on a raised platform in the crossing of the cathedral. The **stalls (55)** were carved, it is thought, by a master carpenter from Norfolk called William Lyngwode. These detailed and elaborate carvings date from the early 14th century. Of particular interest is the carvings on the misericords. The misericord is a medieval curiosity. Each seat is hinged but in the upright position there is a ledge on the underside which can act as a perch when the occupant is in a standing position. Thus, during those parts of the service when standing was required the monks could take some weight off their feet. Nothing was done in medieval times without decoration and on the underside of these seats are some exquisite wood carvings. Each one is unique.

In the centre of the choir is the tomb of **King William II (56),** the only Norman king to be buried at Winchester. He was shot by an arrow during a hunting expedition in the New Forest, by accident, it was said, although there are suspicions to the contrary.

The North Transept

In the **north transept (57)** you may see the original 11th century architectural style and on the west wall is the **Epiphany Chapel (58)** also dating to the 11th century. Backing on to the choir there are wall paintings dating from the 12th century in the chapel of the **Holy Sepulchre (59).** In the summer months when the **crypt (60)** is not flooded it may be possible to tour the crypt and see the mysterious contemplative figure sculpted by Anthony Gormley. As I mentioned earlier, the cathedral was built on a raft and with streams of the Itchen flowing throughout Winchester you don't have to dig down far to find water. The crypt therefore is often under water during the winter months and may not be accessible. On days when it is dry there is a fine sculpture by Anthony Gormley of a standing male figure

holding his hands together as a cup.

Anthony Gormley's contemplative figure in the Crypt

The East End

One of the more surprising monuments here is to **Sir Arnauld de Gaveston (61)** who died around 1302. The name only has resonance today because of the fateful frienship of his son Piers with the young Edward II. Piers de Gaveston was a great friend and favourite of Edward and was rewarded lavishly. He was even created Earl of Cornwall. This alone excited jealousy and resentment among the established nobility but was made worse by Piers de Gaveston's overbearing personality and his tendency to insulting behaviour towards his peers. The barons succeeded in getting him banished in 1308 but Edward brought him back to once more annoy the barons. They exerted further pressure on the king to get him exiled for life and stripped of all

One of the mortuary chests

Above: The tomb of Cardinal Henry Beaufort

his titles at the end of 1311. He did not go far or stay away for long and in 1312 he was back. This time he was unlucky because he was captured by the Earl of Warwick who together with other barons saw to it that he was executed - judicially of course.

Behind the altar is the stone-carved **Great Screen (62)**. It was built by Henry Beaufort and once had statues in the niches. These were destroyed during the reformation, although a few fragments do survive and are on display in the Triforium Gallery.

Perched above the screen on either side of the chancel are six **mortuary chests (63)**. The chests today contain a jumble of bones, none of which at this time of writing, have been properly identified or connected. That is a story in itself as their peace has been disturbed more than once or twice over 1000 years. Originally these Saxon kings were buried in the Old Minster but after that was demolished Bishop Henry of Blois ordered the bones to be re-buried in the new Minster, now the cathedral. They were placed in lead coffins in a passage behind the high altar. This was in 1158 and it appears from recent excavations that there was a raised semi-circular platform upon which the coffins rested. The stones underneath were inscribed with the names of the former kings and bishops.

This romanesque apse was rebuilt in the 14th century and new mortuary chests were made. In 1525 Bishop Foxe oversaw the construction of the present screens and the mortuary chests were placed on top. It is believed that the original chests were too numerous for this display and eight new ones were built and painted and the bones reinterred in the new chest. Some names of former kings and one queen were inscribed on the chests, so today we are able to see the names of Cyneglis, Ethelwulf, Cynewulf, Egbert, Edmund, Eldred, Cnut, Emma,

The chests suffered further disruption during the civil war when Parliamentary troops vandalised the cathedral, scattering the bones from the chests. It is thought that two of these chests were damaged beyond repair and the bones were gathered up and replaced in the six remaining chests, which were themselves repaired and repainted between 1684 and 1693.

The upshot is that these early Tudor chests contain a jumble of Saxon and Danish bones. The mixing up of the bones probably began with the first removal in 1158 and may have been compounded by Bishop Foxe's rationalisation in 1525, only to be made worse by the behaviour of Parliamentary soldiers in 1642. There are rumours, although the cathedral is being tight-lipped about the matter, that the bones are presently under analysis to try to reconnect them to their appropriate identity. At any rate they were removed from display in 2014.

Bishops' Tombs and Chapels

After the Conquest the bishops of Winchester were among the richest and most powerful men in the land. In the 14th century they started the practice of building Chantry Chapels in memory of some of these bishops. There are seven chantry chapels in total and it was expected that a mass would be said daily for the souls of these men. I don't know if the practice continues.

William of Edington (64) served for 20 years until his death in 1366. He was also for a time England's treasurer and Chancellor. His chantry can be found on the south aisle next to the crossing.

He was succeeded by **William of Wykeham (65)** who lived a very long life and died in 1404, serving almost 40 years as bishop. He was also Chancellor of England on two occasions. His origins, on the manor of Wickham just ten miles away, were modest, and he rose to his position of power and wealth on sheer ability. His legacy is fittingly immense. He founded Winchester College and the college at Oxford known as New College. Both institutions are still going strong after 600 years. The chantry for William

Above: The colonnade is all that remains of the Chapter House.

Blow: The south face of the Cathedral, now protected by flying buttresses, once had a cloister surrounding the green.

of Wykeham, as perhaps befits the man who spent so much on the nave is placed between two pillars on the south aisle.

His successor **Henry Beaufort (66)** started life with more advantages but still left his mark. He was a half-brother to King Henry IV and became Chancellor of England on three occasions. He was also one of the few Englishmen to be made a cardinal. He sat as bishop from 1404 until his death in 1447, and that date marked a century of three successive and long-serving powerful bishops. He endowed St Cross Hospital and his legacy was used to build the Great Screen in the cathedral and to build a new shrine to St Swithun. Cardinal Beaufort's painted tomb rest behind the choir.

William Wayneflete (67), who succeeded to the seat in 1447, had been headmaster at Winchester College and his interest in education was such that he founded Magdalen College, Oxford. He died in 1486. His tomb is adjacent to Cardinal Beaufort's in the east end.

He was followed by Peter Courtenay who didn't rate a chapel and then Thomas Langton in 1497. He died in 1501.

Richard Foxe (68) held the see from 1501-1528. The body over his tomb shows an emaciated, skeletal body designed to show that even the mighty come to this in death. He was a secretary of state in Henry VII's government. Bishop Fox'es chantry is on the south side of the choir.

The famous Thomas Wolsey briefly followed him but he gave it up two years later to concentrate on larger affairs of church and state. It is doubtful that the Cardinal spent very much time in Winchester, if any at all. **Stephen Gardiner (69)**, his successor, was quite a force in the realm during a troubled period when the Reformation movement was vying with more conservative forces in the church. Gardiner was a conservative and after 20 years as bishop was deposed by the reforming Edward VI in 1551.

On Mary's accession to the throne two years later he was released from imprisonment in the Tower and reinstated and he held on to office until he died in 1555. His chantry is on the north aisle of the choir.

After this the fashion for chantry chapels waned and later bishops had less to do with government. Men in clerical orders had been essential to government administration during the middle ages, but in the reign of Henry VII those positions began to be filled by men with secular training. Thomas Wriothesley for example, a protege of Stephen Gardiner, rose through the ranks of government to become Chancellor and was created Earl of Southampton. There were more like him and although some later bishops held office, such as Archbishop Laud in the time of Charles 1, the gulf between Church and State widened. Archbishop Laud's term of office ended badly and the convention of drawing men from the church to manage the state died with him.

Two earlier bishops, who were very significant figures have less splendid or even unmarked graves. They were **Henry of Blois (70)** and Peter des Roches. Henry, a younger brother of King Stephen, became bishop when Winchester was still very much a royal centre and London had yet to assert its supremacy as the capital of England. The bishop held estates in most of Hampshire and many other parts of southern England. Henry of Blois was not only powerful through his bloodline but also through his extreme wealth.

He was the builder of **Wolvesey Castle (90)** and was also a patron of the arts. He sponsored many illuminated manuscripts and wall paintings. The Winchester Bible dates from his time and the colours and the fine technique are remarkable. Book production in those days was a massively expensive undertaking and only a man of Henry's wealth could afford this. The Winchester Psalter is also attributed to Henry of Blois and may have

Above: The Deanery

Below: Cheyney Court

been his personal copy. This may be viewed in the **Morley Library (74).**

The treasury of Henry of Blois can be found on the west side of the south transept. The room is now used as a vestry for the choir but in the 12th century was a stronghold for the cathedral's treasury.

The **Tournai Font (54)** also dates from Henry's time.

He was the founder of the hospital at St Cross and the College at Marwell. He also reformed the church at Twyneham and turned it into a monastery for Augustinian canons. This building now survives as Christ Church in the town now named after it on the edge of the New Forest.

He died in 1171 and is buried in the cathedral. His tomb is a plain stone chest with a black marble top, at least it is thought to be his tomb since it dates from the period. The stone coffin itself has no markings.

Peter des Roches was another dominant figure from the 13th century. He was born in Touraine and began his career as a fighting man. Although not of a poor background his origins were modest compared to Henry of Blois, a prince of the realm, but he was able to demonstrate some talent for administration and rose to high rank on ability. King John who placed a premium on such talents quickly promoted him. He seems to have managed the financial affairs of the king although there was no officially-named post at the time. In return he was granted a number of wealthy benefices and in 1204 proposed as Bishop of Winchester, a position he held until his death in 1238. He was a leading political figure during the troubled reigns of King John and his son Henry III. On occasion he led troops in battle and was known as the "Warrior of Winchester." He founded several monasteries, including Hampshire foundations at Titchfield and Netley. Winchester Cathedral is his burial place but the exact location is unknown.

The Shrine of **St. Swithun (71),** as discussed earlier, was a great draw for pilgrims in the middle ages. The possible location of the shrine is marked out and, a modern touch, some Russian Orthodox Church icons have been commissioned to add a spiritual context to the site.

The **south transept (72)**, with its rounded Norman arches shows how the building was originally constructed. In this section is buried here is that gregarious ironmonger and fisherman Izaak Walton. His book *The Compleat Angler* became a classic and if you have read the book it is more about companionship than fishing. He lived to an astonishing age. He was born in Stafford in 1594 and became a successful ironmonger in London. Once he retired from business he set out on a literary career and wrote several biographies. He is of course most remembered for his book on fishing, although he made no claim to be an expert. He was a great friend of George Morley, bishop of Winchester

Prior's Gate

and one of his daughters married a prominent clergyman. In consequence he spent a good part of his later life in Surrey, at Farnham Castle, and in Hampshire at Droxford, where his son-in-law was rector, and finally at Winchester where he died in 1683 in his 90th year.

However, Walton was not all about good fellowship and fishing. He had been a successful businessman and Bishop Morley employed him as his steward and in this role he succeeded in putting to rights the financial affairs of the bishopric which were rather neglected during the Cromwellian interregnum. At his death and Morley's a year later the enterprise was once more on a sound financial footing

He has a chapel dedicated to him in the south transept. It is called the **Fisherman's Chapel (73).** A stained glass window was donated from a fund collected by English and American fisherman depicting Walton in two of his favourite occupations, reading and fishing.

Bishop Morley held the see from 1662 to his death in 1684. During that period he left three important legacies. One of them is the **library (74)**, named after him, which can be reached by a staircase in the south transept. The civil war and the Cromwellian interregnum had left the library in ruins and Morley set about restoring it. The old books and manuscripts which had been salvaged were returned to the shelves and Morley himself donated his own personal library to the collection. It is worth a visit. On display are some other early books, hand written and illuminated with pigments which are still vivid today.

The Cathedral Close

In common with all monastic foundations Winchester was built with cloisters on the south side. Uncommonly, this cathedral dispensed with its cloisters. Only a single arcade from the original **chapter house (75)** survives at Winchester.

The cloisters were gradually removed after the

The house on College Street where Jane Austen spent the last few weeks of her life.

55

The Chamber Court of Winchester College

Below: The College School Room, built in the 16th Century.

dissolution of 1539. Like many other monastic and church buildings in Winchester they became a convenient stone quarry and the cut stone was reused elsewhere. The green area is now simply the site of the former cloisters.

By the twentieth century it became apparent that the destruction of the cloister had left the south wall of the cathedral unsupported so the **flying buttresses (76)** you see today were built only 100 years ago, although they now look to be part of the medieval fabric.

Most of the buildings you now see in the close were built after the middle of the 16th century. The exception is the former Prior's house which is now known as the **Deanery (77).** It had partly residential and partly official functions. The porch has 13th century arches and the Prior's Hall above it has a mid-15th century timber framed roof, The largest part of the building today was rebuilt in the 17th century. After the Priory was dissolved in 1539 the Prior, Walter Kingsmill, kept his job and became the Cathedral Dean and this function has continued. Although this is the seat of the bishop, it is the Dean who is in charge of the management of the cathedral.

In the middle ages there were three very important church figures in Winchester, the bishop of course, the Prior of St Swithun's and the Abbot of Hyde.

The attractive timber framed buildings beside the Prior's Gate are known as **Cheyney Court (78),** It was the court house for the bishop and acquired the name of *Cheyne* or *Cheyney Court*. The name may derive from an old French word *chene*, meaning oak tree. It dates from the 15th century. The building at right angles to the east was originally a barn.

The gate, known as **Prior's Gate (79),** was one of the entrances to the walled compound of the minster. Some of these walls are still preserved as you can see here.

The second gate here, **Kingsgate (80)**, was one of the many entrances to the old city. This gate has a 14th century church dedicated to **St Swithun (81)** above it. The church is usually open and can be reached by a small flight of wooden stairs. It is an appealing and unpretentious chapel.

Winchester College

Once through Kingsgate you are outside the city walls but still on bishop's land and this is where William of Wykeham chose to build his new school. It was dedicated to St Mary but this name is rarely used and the school is known as **Winchester College (82).**

The college is approached down College Street where you can see some 18th century houses on the south side. One of these was the house where **Jane Austen (83)** died after a few weeks of care by the doctor who lived there. Overpowering the street is the **Headmaster's House (84)**. This was built in the 19th century for the headmaster of the college and his family. It is now an administrative building.

The 14th century college presents a walled frontage to the world with a gatehouse designed to keep unwanted people out and the inmates in. Oxford and Cambridge colleges are designed along the same lines, and New College, Oxford, built by Wykeham at the same time as this one, has an almost identical layout.

The wall with a few window openings (all later insertions) was built as the college brewery. In this period ale was essential, as water was likely to be polluted. The Itchen streams which fed the water supply in the south were already contaminated by the townsfolk further north. The brewing of ale, through boiling the mash and fermentation usually killed off fatal microbes and rendered a safe low alcohol drink for men women and children.

Winchester College offers guided tours on most days and times are posted on the notice board outside. This is the only way visitors may see the college. You may have time to visit **Wolvesey Castle (90)** before the next tour.

The **gatehouse (82)** opens into a small

The 17th. Century Bishop's Palace

courtyard for the business buildings of the college. The brewhouse, now a library, and probably a granary and a slaughterhouse and other storage buildings.

A second gateway leads to a **chamber court (85)** which offered accommodation for the scholars, the warden and the master. At the south end of the courtyard is the **chapel (86)**. A refectory can be reached up a flight of stairs. The courtyard and the refectory have been used in various Harry Potter films.

The final quadrangle is a **cloister (87)** intended for study and quiet contemplation. Some of the supporting columns are now leaning at an angle after 600 years. One assumes that the structure of the building is being monitored.

The cloisters were used as classrooms during the summer months when, before the days of insulation, the interior rooms became too hot and stifling.

Within the cloister is a 15th century **chantry chapel (88)**, built through the bequest of John Fromond, a former steward of the college. It has two stories. The upper hall reached by a spiral staircase was intended as the lodging for the chantry priest but has had various uses since. The outside of the building has carved figures to represent the officials of the college.

Just to the east of this is a **schoolroom (89)** built in the 16th century. It is still in use.

That is the original college. Over the centuries it has much expanded and most of the properties surrounding the college have been acquired for accommodation or administration, and indeed elsewhere in the city. All students are boarders; Winchester College does not take day students. It is now one of the most successful and prestigious schools in the country. It was not always so. In the first part of the 18th century the number of commoners declined to 8 and was gradually rescued in the second half of that century. This period was not without incident and there were periodic outbreaks of violence involving the boys of the college with several reports of street fighting between the commoners and Winchester resident.

The college moved into a period of prosperity in the 19th century as may be evidenced by the splendid Headmaster's house on College street.

William of Wykeham

William of Wykeham was born not too many miles from here on the manor of Wickham. His father who worked the land on the manor was most likely not a poor peasant but neither was he a landowner, so William can be said to have come from humble origins. His father John, who carried the surname Long, was probably above average in height, as was his son. William was obviously exceptionally bright and it was common enough for intelligent boys to be taken on by the church.

William quickly demonstrated his ability first working for the constable of Winchester Castle and then for the Crown on various building projects including Windsor Castle, By 1361, approaching the age of 40, he became a royal secretary managing the king's finances and only two years later was made Lord Privy Seal

In a manner which might today strike us as odd, he was paid for these services indirectly, through the income of several religious benefices. At the time he was created Bishop of Winchester in 1366 he was Archdeacon of Lincoln, held two benefices and eleven prebends, giving him an income of £800 a year, a huge sum in those days. In the following year he was made Chancellor although he lost that position a few years later in 1371. These were uncertain years for William and at one point he lost his estates to a rival, but these were restored a few months after Richard II came to the throne. William was created Chancellor again in 1389 and served in this position until 1391.

After this he devoted himself to the two great college foundations which of course have prospered to this day.

In 1382 he acquired the land beyond the minster walls to found his school, known as Winchester College. By itself this was not an unusual act for a man in his position, but this college was to be part of a grand plan whereby the Winchester school fed into his Oxford college, usually known as New College. Accordingly both foundations were for 70 scholars. Neither college carries its full name in common usage. Both were dedicated to St Mary and are more properly named ST Mary's College, but the college in Winchester is always known as Winchester College and the one in Oxford as New College. Their simultaneous foundation meant that they were both designed by one builder, William de Wyneford, and both conform to the same design. Some originality also lies in he formal introduction by William of Wykeham of a two tier concept of education.

Winchester college opened in 1394 and was probably completed in its first phase a decade later. Over the 600 years of its existence it has expanded greatly on its campus and through houses all along Kingsgate and the surrounding streets. These pupils are known as commoners

Two views of the ruins of Wolvesey Castle

and are fee paying. This number originally started at 10 but has increased enormously and the demand is very high. Fees for commoners are £34,000 a year. The 70 scholars are still supported.

Wolvesey Castle

The large building attached to the chapel of Wolvesey Castle is the present **Bishop's Palace (91)**. It was built through an endowment in the legacy of Bishop Morley who died in 1684. **Wolvesey Castle (90)** had been damaged by the Parliamentary army during the civil war, but once Cromwell came to power he took steps to ensure that it would never be used again for defensive purposes. Demolition work began in late 1650 and continued into the following year. It was difficult work because the walls were very thick and at the restoration in 1660 the work was still not complete. What you see today is the remnant of that time with a few 20th century reinforcements to make the building safe. The chapel was not destroyed and is now incorporated

Wolvesey Castle: an aerial view.

into the present palace.

The early bishops were great and powerful lords and the Bishop of Winchester was one of the greatest, and certainly the richest, in the land. He was able to maintain a palace at Winchester, another at Farnham in Surrey, close to London and a summer palace at Bishops Waltham a few miles east of Winchester in Bere Forest.

Here at Winchester Henry of Blois built Wolvesey Castle, a sumptuous fortified palace. The ruins remain and are today managed by English Heritage. Admission is free and the premises are open daily from April 1st to November 2nd.

Wolvesey Castle is also on the route of Walk 5. It may be convenient to take it in here.

Return along College Street and through Kingsgate and continue west outside the cathedral close walls along St. Swithun's Street.

St. Swithun's Street

The views of the houses along this street are restricted by the high wall on the north side which surrounds the cathedral close.

At the corner of St. Swithun and Great Minster you will encounter **Christ's Hospital (92)**, founded by Peter Symonds.

Peter Symonds was a stepson of Richard Bethell, the Winchester merchant who had acquired Hyde Abbey and built his house there so it is not surprising to discover that stone from Hyde Abbey were used in the construction of the almshouses named after the founder. Peter Symonds was a wealthy merchant and spent the major part of his life making money in London, where he was a member of the Mercer's Company. He died in 1586 leaving a substantial bequest to the foundation of the almshouses just outside the cathedral on what is now called Symonds Street. The almshouses provided for six poor single men and four poor children. Quite how this mix was determined is not apparent. An Oxford and a Cambridge scholar was supported by the foundation and possibly these candidates came from the boys taken into the almshouse. As

Christ's Hospital on Symond's Street
Below: Great Minster Street

you may see from the inscription over the central doorway the almshouses were completed in 1607.

St. Thomas Street

If you wish to climb a little higher to the

Part of St. Thomas Street

corner of St. Thomas Street there is a large **18th century mansion (93)** facing the intersection which is reputed to be the house built for the Duke of York in the late 17th century. This dates to the period when Charles II was planning to re-develop Winchester as a royal city. The Duke of York succeeded his brother as King James II. The house has since been divided and altered but you can still view it as a once splendid town house.

St. Thomas Street itself was much favoured by the well-to-do for their residences as a much healthier part of Winchester than lower down near the river streams. Accordingly there are some impressive 18th century mansions here with impressive views over the city - at least for the occupants..

The street begins with a small range of cottages followed by three large separated mansion houses. The middle one of the three, Mulberry House, once had a mulberry treet said to have been planted by Charles II. This tree was uprooted in the great storm of 1987. Opposite this house is Mason's Yard, presently converted to residences but believed to have been a stable block for Mulberry House. Beyond Mason's Yard was once the site for the church which gave its name to the street. By the 19th century the church required serious repair so moves were made to build a new church which accordingly opened in 1847 on Southgate Street, next to Serle's House. The only evidence of the former church is the wall and an open green space.

Cut down the narrow Minster Lane to St. Swithun Street, fronted by the high wall round the Cathedral Close. A short dog leg will bring you to the front of the Cathedral on Great Minster Street.

This concludes this walk. The Cathedral Visitor Centre has a shop and offers refreshment.

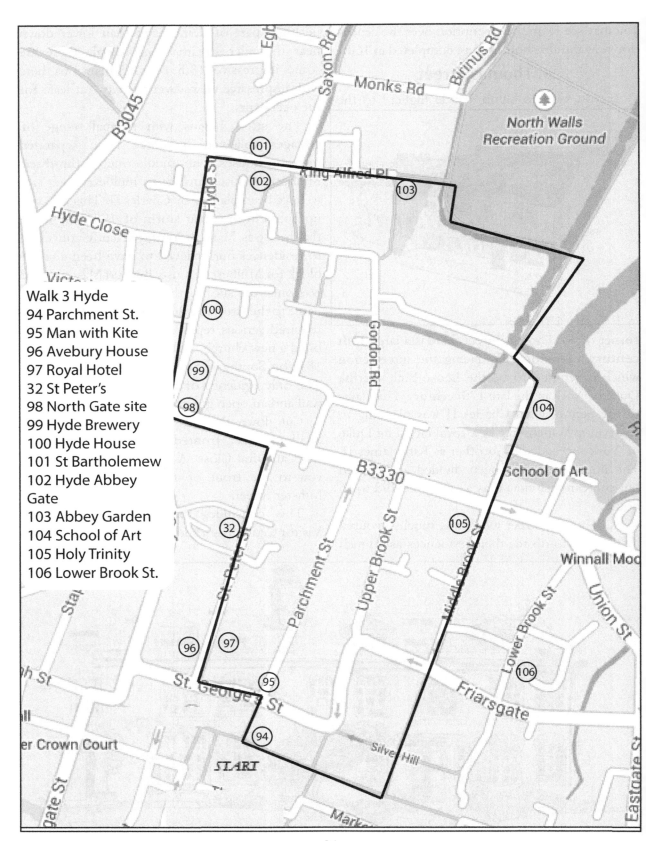

Walk 3 Hyde
94 Parchment St.
95 Man with Kite
96 Avebury House
97 Royal Hotel
32 St Peter's
98 North Gate site
99 Hyde Brewery
100 Hyde House
101 St Bartholemew
102 Hyde Abbey
Gate
103 Abbey Garden
104 School of Art
105 Holy Trinity
106 Lower Brook St.

Walk Three:
Hyde and North Winchester

This walk will take you through north Winchester and to Hyde beyond the north walls. From the middle ages it was always a district where people lived and worked and there are therefore fewer institutional or commercial buildings here. This was the Winchester of artisans as the street names used to tell you what sort of business happened there. Fleshmonger's Street has today been given the more stately name of St Peter's Street. Shield maker's street is now Upper Brook, Middle Brook is the new name for Wunegrestret and Tanner's Street is now Lower Brook Street. Also to be found was a Tailor's Street (Snidelingstret) a Shoemaker's Street and a Wood Street. This was not necessarily the nicest part of Winchester. In medieval times it was noisy, smelly and dirty.

Today it is clean, quiet and respectable and considerably changed. The streets have not changed for centuries and the steps you tread today are the on the same paths as our ancestors.

It has also been more subject to clearance and renewal than the parts you have just visited and most of the buildings are 19th and 20th century.

This tour starts at the High Street - Parchment Street intersection and proceeds north. Turn up St George's Street to St. Peter's Street and continue north. Another dog leg along the North Walls to Hyde Street where the old North gate used to stand and north again to King Alfred's Place. This will take you through the site of the former Hyde Abbey, then across the meadows to Park Road. Head south from here to return to the city.

The time for this walk is about an hour.

Parchment Street

Parchment Street (94) branches from the High Street as a short pedestrian passage, but it starts to take on its own character once across St George's Street. If you look up you will see a metal bridge straddling the street with a **man flying a kite (95)** walking across it. It was created by Marzia Colonna an Italian-born artist who has her studio in Dorset. It was commissioned in 2009 and she is the latest distinguished sculptor to have work installed in the city.

The section of Parchment Street that follows is home to interesting shops that provide goods and services out of the mainstream. There are no chain stores or high volume shops along this street and this is part of its charm. Beyond the shopping area are terraces of 19th and 20th century cottages and town houses, all neatly kept.

This street was once home to a new hospital, opened in 1759, but there were so many problems with water supply and sewage disposal in central Winchester that a century later the hospital moved out of town to its present location on the Romsey Road.

From the corner walk up St George's Street to St. Peter's Street. This block was redeveloped in the 20th century.

Parchment Street

St. Peter's Street

On this street are two large town houses, once homes to wealthy Winchester families.

Avebury House (96) is a large city centre mansion built in an age when wealthy families chose to live within the city walls. The house was originally built in 1690 with the south wing dating from the 18th century. There are 19th century modifications. It is now used for offices.

The Royal Hotel (97) opposite opened as a hotel in 1859 and was much modified in that century. The original house may date to the same period as Avebury House.

Further north is **St Peter's Roman Cathlolic Church (32)**. this is a 20th century building although it does incorporate a 12th century door in the north wall salvaged from the Magdalen Hospital, a leper hospital about one mile to the east of Winchester.

In 1109 the monks of the New Minster, next door to the Cathedral, acquired Hyde Meadow and in the following year began to populate this area north of the city walls. There they built a large and prosperous abbey which was bounded by Monks Place at the north, Hyde Street to the west and streams of the Itchen to the east and south. Excavations have revealed a large minster church with cloisters and living quarters in the eastern section. To the west there was an inner courtyard which may have contained some of the functional buildings, such as storehouses, brewery,, buttery, kitchens and so forth. The gatehouse, which survived demolition in the 16th century was the entrance to this courtyard.

Above: Two house frontages on St. Peter's Street.

Right: Part of the Royal Hotel.

Houses on Hyde Street

The "Counting House" from the old Hyde Brewery

Below: Counting House doorway and a house on Hyde Street

Hyde

Hyde Street begins where the **North Gate (98)** once controlled entrance to the city. That, together with the city walls, has long gone and only a plaque remains to mark the spot. There was once a large brewery on the right but only a single building, known as the **Counting House (99)**, remains. The red brick building is not unattractive. It is believed that the brewery started on this site in the early part of the 18th century and had its hey-day in the 19th century. The brewery operated as such until 1925 when the brewing was transferred to another site and these premises were used as a distribution depot. It finally closed in 1997 and the site was redeveloped.

A little further north, a large house with a Dutch gable roof fronts the street with a large yard surrounded by brick walls. The Hyde Abbey site was granted to Richard Bethell after the

Above: Hyde Abbey Gate

Below: St. Bartholemew's Church

Page 71: Part of the Hyde Abbey Gardens

dissolution and he built a mansion here known as **Hyde House (100)**. Bethell came to Winchester in 1520 from Flintshire, apparently at the request of the Abbot of Hyde, although for what purpose is unknown. He settled near Hyde and in 1536 leased the manor of Woodmancott (one of the abbey's manors). He was a mercer (cloth dealer) and was described by contemporaries as a man of great substance. There is certainly proof of this. After the dissolution he was able to purchase the abbey grounds and the tenements in the Hyde district for £110, thus becoming a substantial landlord. This was not a small sum; £5 a year would have kept a family in relative comfort in the 1540s. He was elected Mayor of Winchester in 1553 and became one of Winchester's MPs the following year. He died in 1570 and was succeeded by his son William.

Hyde House was built in the middle of the 16th century although it must have been remodelled or rebuilt on occasion during its history. The part which does survive, apparently one wing of the mansion, looks to me like a late 17th century building.

On the other side of the street are some large 18th century mansions.

Turn to the east at King Alfred Place where you will first see the church of **St Bartholemew (101)** on the north side. The church dates from a similar period to the abbey foundation and was the church for the villagers who settled around Hyde, many of whom would have found employment in the abbey. Rebuilding and modification has taken place over the centuries, Some parts of the abbey, for example have been incorporated in the church, and the chancel and north side of the church was rebuilt in Victorian times.

On the right you can discover the old **gatehouse (102)** to the abbey and the only part of Hyde Abbey which has survived more-or-less intact. Why this part was preserved is not known for certain but quite possibly Richard Bethell kept it as a gatehouse to his own new estate.

The building is well-maintained and some

Two views of the Itchen streams in Hyde

On page 73: Part of the School of Art

presentation boards describe the history of the abbey and show plans for the original conventual buildings and the territory it once covered.

Continue along King Alfred Place, a 20th century development. This street is built over the site of the **abbey church (103)** but the end of the street opens up to a park beginning with a ground plan of the area once taken up by the east end of the church. This is an imaginative presentation. Columns are symbolised by holly bushes surrounded by a metal cage with circular aluminium bands. Further to the east the buttresses are similarly depicted but with rectangular bands. There are three gravestone slabs, marked only with a cross to symbolise the final resting places of King Alfred, his queen Eahlswith and their son King Edward. Their remains are not actually there and their bones will have to await further discovery, but the symbolism is important.

Even this outline of the Lady Chapel, only a small section of the church, may give you some concept of what must once have been an impressive building. These gardens are a highly creative way of acknowledging the past.

The gardens open up into a park and recreational fields. The River Itchen runs through several channels here and the banks are all man made. The path will lead you to the University campus on Park Road This was originally **Winchester School of Art (104)** and is now the art and design college within the University of Southampton. The buildings are modern but quite pleasing to the eye.

Middle Brook Street

Take the road south and cross into Middle Brook Street, once known by its Saxon name of Wunegrestret. On the corner stands **Holy Trinity Church (105)**, a mid-Victorian creation in a gothic style. Almost all the building along this ancient street are 19th and 20th century in origin,so although you are walking along a street that was laid out 2000 years ago, there is little

Top: Holy Trinity Church

Bottom: 16th century building on Middle Brook Street

left to remind us of the many developments have come and gone in that period. Despite the recent origin of these buildings nothing seems out of place here and it is perhaps part of the appeal of cities like Winchester that buildings from different periods can live comfortably side by side. Winchester has museums, but the town itself is not a museum. It is a place where people live and work and adapt to changing times. That said, Winchester has been very successful in adapting its ancient city, largely by maintaining low rise development throughout.

One building that stands out as a survivor of all this development is the timber framed building on the corner. It is believed to be of 16th century origin but was largely rebuilt in the 19th century.

The land to the east was occupied by the Franciscan Friars until the monastic dissolution. Their church was dedicated to their patron St. Francis. As a mendicant order they had few assets compared to the monasteries and the inventory taken in 1538 revealed lttle more than household necessities and kitchen implements. The house was closed down in that year and the land granted to Winchester College. The street and car park known as Friarsgate is the only sign that they once existed in this part of Winchester.

There are three Brook Streets - Upper, Middle and Lower. Each of them had streams of the Itchen running through them. They probably still do, except that they are now underground.

One consequence of this industrial activity in the north of Winchester was that all the effluent was carried downstream, and even in the middle ages this was recognised as a danger to health. And so breweries became an essential component of any institution built to the south and indeed, when Winchester College was built in 1391, almost the first building was a brewery, as noted earlier.

One of the advantages of late 20th century development is that archaeologists were allowed in first to excavate the site for any earlier evidence of settlement. One important dig was conducted along **Lower Brook Street (106)** (formerly Tanner's Street) in the post war years to reveal the medieval (and earlier) settlement. The **City Museum (39)** has more information.

These two drawings, one from the 19th century and another drawn about 100 years ago, will give you some idea of the change that has taken place in this street.

In the 19th century the stream is still running down the street as it did in medieval times. By the 20th century a paved street has covered this over. nevertheless, virtually every building has since been replaced by something more modern.

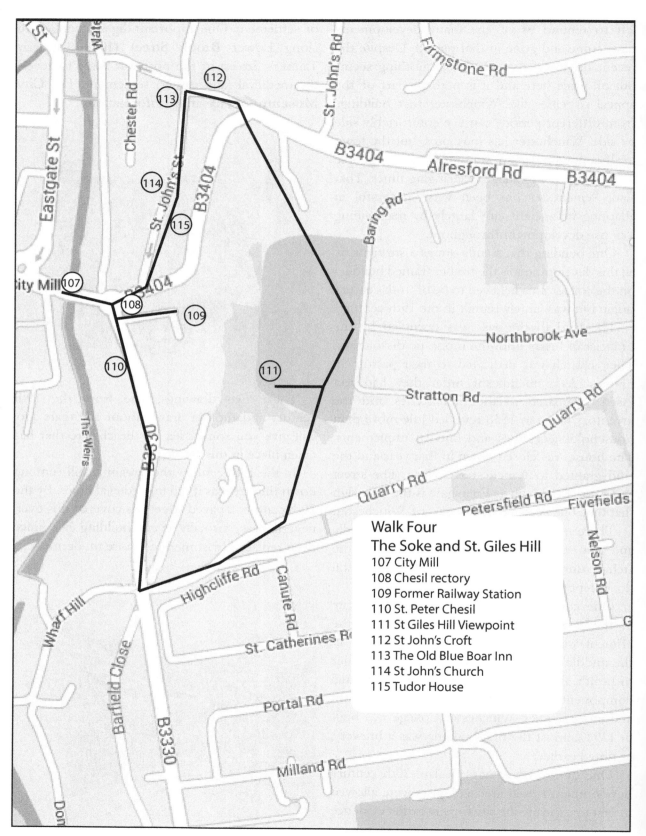

Walk Four
The Soke and St. Giles Hill
107 City Mill
108 Chesil rectory
109 Former Railway Station
110 St. Peter Chesil
111 St Giles Hill Viewpoint
112 St John's Croft
113 The Old Blue Boar Inn
114 St John's Church
115 Tudor House

Walk Four: The Soke

This walk will take you outside the ancient city to the eastern bank of the Itchen known as the Soke. It was under the jurisdiction of the bishop rather than the city corporation.

This walk will involve some steep climbing up St Giles Hill.

The route will take you across the bridge and south along Chesil Street. Turn left at East Hill and veer left at Quarry Road and shortly leave this road for a footpath and a steady but steep climb up the hill. The viewpoint about two thirds of the way up is worth the effort. You may continue to the top of the hill and down the other side to come out on the Magdalen Hill Road. The last part of this walk will take you down Blue Ball Hill and St John's Street.

Allow an hour to an hour and a half.

The 18th century City Mill

The City Mill

Standing on the bridge, watching the river churning under the mill, gives us a strong clue as to why people settled Winchester in the first place. Here was an abundant water supply to power several mills and the industrial processes of medieval England. This mill is a survivor. It was rebuilt in its present form in 1743 to replace the medieval mill that was once here. It is probable that there were several predecessors of that mill. The **City Mill (107)** is owned by the National Trust, who have recently restored it to a fully operating corn mill., so it has now been grinding flour for about a decade since restoration.

I can recall staying here in the 1950s when it was a Youth Hostel. In those days when I was a teenager and roads were relatively traffic free I was able to roam England on my bicycle and find ready and cheap accommodation run by the Youth Hostel Association. On one of

Bridge Street.

Below: Chesil Rectory.   *Opposite page: Chesil Street*

those occasions I came down from my home in Buckighamshire to explore this part of the world.

Once you cross the bridge you leave the old city of Winchester and enter what was called the Soke. The people who lived here were extra-mural and were not under the jurisdiction of the town authorities. Instead they were governed by the bishop. In practical ways that may have

Chesil Street.

Below: St. Peter Chesil, now a theatre

resulted in lower taxes.

The river was once much wider but the eastern bank has been built up and developed in the 18th and 19th centuries.

Chesil

The eastern bank of the river is now built-up to the edge, and the river channel is walled on either side but at one time the river channel was wider and there was a gravel bank for the mooring of boats - a chesil. In time this was corrupted to Cheesehill and the street was so-named. Chesil Street is now the restored name.

The 15th century house standing by itself and now set back some distance from the river at one time considered itself to be on the river bank. It probably began its life as a merchant's house with storage and trading areas at ground level and with living accommodation on the upper floors. The location beside the beach was convenient for loading and unloading boats. As it was on the bishops land, even though the house would have been built at the merchant's expense, the property would always belong to the ecclesiastics. Therefore, when the monasteries were dissolved in 1538 this became crown property. However, in 1554 it was donated by Queen Mary to the city corporation to partly offset the expense of her wedding to King Phillip of Spain in 1554. It is now a restaurant called the **Chesil Rectory (108)**. For one period in its history it was used as a rectory for St Peter's Church.

A little beyond this building you can find the site of a railway station and a tunnel under St Giles Hill. This was a very late railway, the **Didcot, Newbury and Southampton Railway (109)**, fully opened in 1891. It was the ambition of the directors to create a north-south route from Southampton to Manchester but all they succeeded in doing was linking a few villages to larger centres. To bring the line to Winchester necessitated building a tunnel. You can see the

A view from St. Giles Hill

When St. Giles Hill was developed in the ate 19th century, large proerties such as this one commanded the view.

Below: St. John's Croft

entrance here where it once opened up to a station. The tunnel is now used for storage. The railway was never economic. In 1923 it became part of the Great Western Group and in 1948 was absorbed in to the western region of British railways. It was closed in 1962.

From here walk south along Chesil Street.

The church of **St. Peter (110)** dates from the 13th century. It is a modest building with a squat tower and it seated about 300 in the 19th century. In the 1960s the building was acquired by the Winchester Dramatic Society as a home for their productions and was converted into a small theatre. The company stages six plays each year.

After the church the road narrows and the houses are modest in scale. Most are late 19th or 20th century brick cottages, but there are some 18th century cottages on the east side.

St. Giles Hill

Turn left at East Hill and start climbing. The road forks at Quarry Road. Take Quarry Road. On your left you will find a green Public Footpath sign. Follow this and the path will take you northwards across a green park area over **St Giles Hill (111)**. Steps have been cut into the side of the hill and there are resting points on the way up. I didn't count the steps, but there are many. Before you reach the top there is a path on your left to take you a short walk to the viewpoint. On a clear day, and in the morning with the sun at your back, the view is very rewarding and all the landmarks are noted on display boards.

Continue the climb. Near the top you will come to an avenue of trees. There are some spacious 19th century mansions on the right hand side.

Development only became possible after the middle of the 19th century when church reforms

The Old Blue Boar Inn

St. John's Church

Below: The Tudor House on St. John's Street

released land holdings from the control of the bishop and the Church Commissioners were free to sell it. The city corporation purchased some of the land in 1878 and Lord Northbrook donated his landholdings on the hill to the city in 1894.

The area was attractive to the wealthier Winchester merchants who could afford the view and maintain carriage and horses to take them up and down the hill. The very large house on the corner of Northbrook Avenue, is now divided into several properties, but the external architecture still tells us that this was once a large family home with room for stables and other outbuildings and a platoon of servants to maintain the house.

St. Giles Fair

St Giles down was not always covered with trees and houses as it is now. In the middle ages it was the site of one of the great annual fairs of England, beginning as a one day event on the feast of St Giles in the time of William Rufus. This grant was extended to six days by Henry I and to sixteen in the time of Henry II. Further increases extended the fair to twenty-four days, practically a month. It must have been a huge event. Where the proceeds were recorded in the 13th century the average take was about £125, a small enough figure to us today, but a huge amount in the middle of the 13th century.

This was the bishop's land and he was the main beneficiary of this trade. London merchants made a point of setting up booths here every September and traders from abroad also made their way to Winchester. There are records of merchants from Flanders, most parts of France, Spain and a few from Italy. The merchants brought finished goods made of brass and iron, cloth and fine textiles, dyes were on sale, horses and other livestock, wine was imported from Gascony, wool and hides came from across England. In addition there are reports of exotic animals such as apes and bears being brought here for sale. Buyers came to purchase the highly-prized English wool. In all probability there was nothing here that was not a feature of life in medieval England.

The merchants of Winchester were somewhat the losers. The bishop had obtained an order that prevented anyone from selling goods outside the fair within a radius of seven leagues (about 20 miles) effectively shutting down their businesses for a month. Only Southampton, just outside the limit could benefit, as indeed they did by offering inducements to foreign traders to spend their money within Southampton's walls before they set out for Winchester, and some apparently never made it as far as Winchester, having spent their money in Southampton.

The Hundred Years war had an impact on the fair. The Gascon wine trade was curtailed and trade from Normandy and France ceased altogether. Once it lost its status as a great international fair, English traders stopped coming from further afield and by the later middle ages the fair had dwindled in importance to something like a county fair. Receipts by the middle of the 14th century had fallen to about one quarter of their 13th century high point.

Today the hill is partly residential development and partly a park. Only the name remains to remind us of the once annual fair.

Descend across the down in a north easterly direction. The path down zig-zags but try to keep an eastern bearing so that you don't come out too low down. The exit point should bring you out opposite Blue Ball Hill.

Cross the Magdalen Hill road at a safe point and you will get a good view of the city from here. Magdalen Hill is so named because this road will take you about a mile or so eastwards to the site of the former St. Mary Magdalen Hospital. This was a leper hospital and the sufferers from leprosy were kept apart from the town because of fear of contagion. The institution operated, although not as a leper hospital, until 1788 when it was demolished.

From a green on Blue Boar Hill there is a pleasant view over the city to the west.

The church tower in the foreground is the church of St John the Baptist, which was founded here in the early 12th century.

Although outside the city walls, this part of Winchester is quite old.

St. John's Street

The name Blue Ball Hill is most likely a corruption of Blue Boar Hill, named after the ancient inn of that name. On the right is an 18th century house from the Queen Anne period, known as **St John's Croft (112)**. Ahead is an

interesting medieval survivor, which is still called the **Old Blue Boar Inn (113)**, although it has not functioned as an inn for over two centuries.

On the corner stands a 14th century hall type house. It is believed to have been built in 1340. It was known as the Blue Boar Inn and in later times as the Old Blue Boar, and it is highly probable that it had other names during its long history; it was, for example, called the White Boar in the 15th century. The building is a private residence and is well maintained. It has a tile roof although the original was certainly thatch. It had long since ceased to be an alehouse by the 19th century.

The little triangular green here offers a good view of the city.

St. John's Street, once a through road on the eastern bank of the Itchen, known as the Pilgrim's Way, was a natural location for an inn such as the Blue Boar and a church. The church of **St John the Baptist (114)**, founded before 1142, is one of Winchester's oldest surviving churches. Astonishing as it may appear to us today, Wichester had 54 churches in medieval times. This number had been reduced to 26 by 1500 and 100 years after that had been reduced to 12. From this cull, only St Peter Chesil and St John in the Soke remained. On weekdays, if someone is in attendance, the church will be open and is worth a visit. The interior is quite spacious using the rounded arches of the period. There are some medieval paintings on the walls.

The church was apparently used as the collegiate chapel of Winchester College at the end of the 14th century while the new chapel for the college was under construction.

St John Street is now mainly 19th century terraced cottages, but one 16th century timber framed hall remains. It is known as the **Tudor House (115).**

Return to the starting point at the bridge.

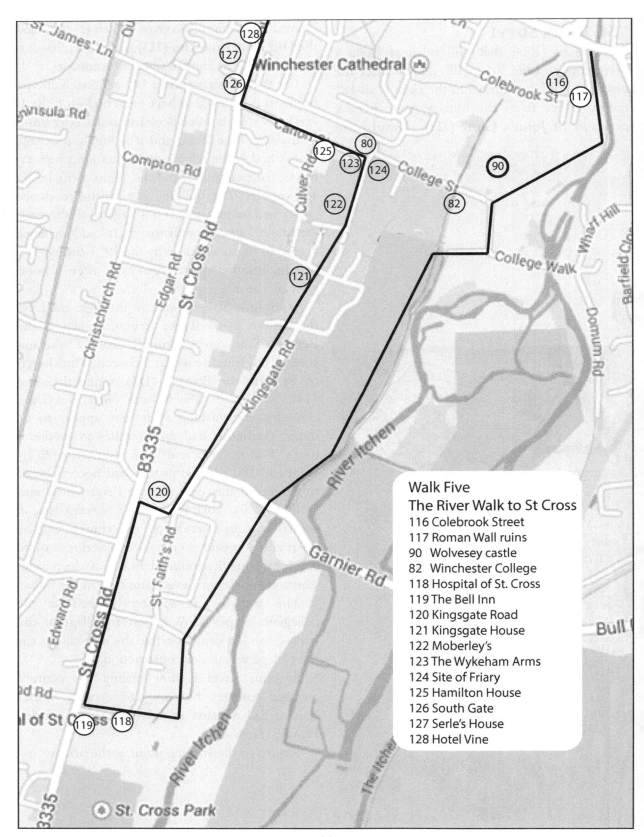

Walk Five
The River Walk to St Cross
116 Colebrook Street
117 Roman Wall ruins
90 Wolvesey castle
82 Winchester College
118 Hospital of St. Cross
119 The Bell Inn
120 Kingsgate Road
121 Kingsgate House
122 Moberley's
123 The Wykeham Arms
124 Site of Friary
125 Hamilton House
126 South Gate
127 Serle's House
128 Hotel Vine

Walk Five: St Cross and Southgate

This walk is the longest of the five and will take you south to the medieval hospital of St. Cross, still committed to its original purpose after 850 years.

On a good day this is a pleasant walk along the river bank, a visit to the hospital and a return along Kingsgate Road, up Canon street to Southgate and concluding at the High Street. The distance is about 3.5 miles.

John Keats

John Keats, the gifted English Romantic poet, arrived in Winchester on August 12th in 1819 after a visit to Shanklin in the Isle of Wight. Apart from an interest in the ancient city he apparently assumed that he would be able to find a library there. Indeed Winchester did have two important libraries, but both were closed to outsiders. In this letter he describes his first impressions to his sister, Fanny.

29 August 1819
You must forgive me for suffering so long a space to elapse between the dates of my letters. It is more than a fortnight since I left Shanklin, chiefly for the purpose of being near a tolerable Library, which after all is not to be found in this place. However we like it very much: it is the pleasantest Town I ever was in, and has the most recommendations of any. There is a fine Cathedrall which to me is always a source of amusement, part of it built 1400 years ago; and the more modern by a magnificent Man, you may have read of in our History, called William of Wickham. The whole town is beautifully wooded – From the Hill at the eastern extremity you see a prospect of Streets, and old Buildings mixed up with Trees. Then there are the most beautiful streams about I ever saw – full of Trout. There is the Foundation of St Croix about half a mile in the fields – a charity greatly abused. We have a Collegiate School, a roman catholic School; a chapel ditto and a Nunnery! And what improves it all is, the fashionable inhabitants are all gone to Southampton.

It is not known precisely where he stayed but literary detectives have mined his letters for clues and there is some consensus that he found lodgings on Colebrook Street. From there it was not difficult to find the path along the river, which he did one Sunday on the 19th of September. On September 19th Keats took a walk along the River Itchen. You can follow in his footsteps today. When he came back he wrote down the poem he had composed. We know it as the Ode to Autumn, one of his more famous poems and, though he did not intend it, one of his last. Two days later he wrote to his friend John Reynolds and described the effect the scene had upon him:

How beautiful the season is now – How fine the air. A temperate sharpness about it. Really, without joking, chaste weather – Dian skies – I never lik'd stubble fields so much as now – Aye better than the chilly green of the Spring. Somehow a stubble-plain looks warm – in the same way that some pictures look warm – This struck me so much in my Sunday's walk that I composed upon it.

Season of mists and mellow fruitfulness
Close bosom-friend of the maturing sun
Conspiring with him how to load and bless
With fruit the vines that round the thatch-eaves run;
To bend with apples the moss'd cottage-trees,
And fill all fruit with ripeness to the core;
To swell the gourd, and plump the hazel shells
With a sweet kernel; to set budding more,
And still more, later flowers for the bees,

The River Itchen near St. Cross
Above: Winchester College Chapel

Until they think warm days will never cease,
For Summer has o'er-brimm'd their clammy cells.
Who hath not seen thee oft amid thy store?
Sometimes whoever seeks abroad may find
Thee sitting careless on a granary floor,
Thy hair soft-lifted by the winnowing wind;
Or on a half-reap'd furrow sound asleep,
Drows'd with the fume of poppies, while thy hook
Spares the next swath and all its twined flowers:
And sometimes like a gleaner thou dost keep
Steady thy laden head across a brook;
Or by a cider-press, with patient look,
Thou watchest the last oozings hours by hours.
Where are the songs of Spring? Ay, where are they?
Think not of them, thou hast thy music too,-
While barred clouds bloom the soft-dying day,
And touch the stubble-plains with rosy hue;
Then in a wailful choir the small gnats mourn
Among the river sallows, borne aloft
Or sinking as the light wind lives or dies;
And full-grown lambs loud bleat from hilly bourn;
Hedge-crickets sing; and now with treble soft
The red-breast whistles from a garden-croft;
And gathering swallows twitter in the skies.

He revised the poem the following year when it was published. It has always been held in high regard as one of the great poems of the English language.

Ironically, although the poem exudes contentment, this was a troubled time in Keats' life. He was in financial difficulties and the life of a poet, then as now, was not a good way to earn a living. In 1820 he contracted tuberculosis and his health deteriorated. He was advised in September, a year after he had composed the *Ode to Autumn*, to move to a warmer climate. He set sail for Rome and died there on 21st February 1821. He lived only for 25 years.

In Keats' Footsteps

Wherever Keats may have stayed, in **Colebrook Street (116)** or Paternoster Row, will not be found as this area has been wholly redeveloped. We can start this walk by the bridge which provides a comfortable footpath south alongside the river. After a few steps you will come across some remnants of the actual East gate to the city which was managed by the Nuns of St Mary's Abbey. There are also some visible remains of the **Roman wall (117)**. The footpath will take you alongside the walls of **Wolvesey Castle (90)** and at College Street you will be able to turn right and into the castle grounds.

Admission to the castle is now free and through a narrow path between the present **Bishop's Palace** and the school playing fields. Work on the castle began in 1138 at the direction of Bishop Henry of Blois. It was intended as a palace and the principal residence of the bishop. In those days, particularly as this was a period of civil war with his brother Stephen and his cousin Matilda in a struggle for the throne, fortification was essential. The bishop was not rooted to Winchester. He had a castle at Farnham in Surrey and a summer palace at Bishops Waltham as well as many manor houses for himself across his territory.

It continued to be used by the bishops until the civil war of the 17th century. After the Parliamentary forces gained control of Winchester in 1646 Wolvesey was reduced to a ruin so that it could not be used again as a castle. The chapel survived and is still attached to the new bishop's palace which was built after the civil war.

Enough of the ruins remain, with helpful notice boards provided by English Heritage, to gather some concept of the scale and layout of the palace.

Retrace your steps to the south and join College Walk which skirts the College grounds and continues to the south. This path will take

St. Cross Chapel

Above: A view from St Catherine's Hill

you along Keat's walk about a mile until you come to **St Cross Hospital (118).**

A History:

the Hospital of Saint Cross

When John Keats came here in 1819 he noted that it was "a charity much abused"

The hospital was founded in 1136 by Bishop Henry of Blois and it was well-endowed from the outset. He provided for the accommodation of thirteen poor and infirm old men who could no longer work for their living. In addition bread and ale were to be provided at the gate for 100 poor men daily. Today we notice that there is no mention of women in any of the charters and it must be assumed that it was taken for granted that women were cared for by other means. Since the 100 men were permitted to take away food and drink it was probably expected that they would take the remnants to their families.

After the death of Bishop Henry in 1173 the management of the hospital opened into dispute between the bishop and the hospitallers and here began a lengthy struggle where at times judgement went to the bishop and at others judgement went to the hospitallers. In consequence the hospital did not get steady management or even management in its best interests for many years. There were absentee masters at times who were content to cream off the income and paid little attention to the founding function of the hospital and by the 14th century people were not being fed at the gate and the buildings were crumbling.

William of Wykeham, who became bishop in 1366, turned his attention to the hospital in 1368. It took him about seven years of sustained effort to gain full control and set the hospital back on its proper course. The poor were now fed daily and the buildings began to be repaired.

Good management continued with Wykeham's successor, Cardinal Henry Beaufort who further willed an extension to the hospital with provision for a further 24 resident brethren.

These intentions were implemented later in the century.

The hospital was one of those institutions not subject to confiscation during the time of monastic dissolution and it continues to this day. It was not however to be free of scandal and in the 19th century matters came to a head once more.

While Keats was walking past this amiable place in 1819 the master was one Francis North, presented with the job in 1808 by his father Brownlow North, Bishop of Winchester. The Bishop of Winchester, with an income far greater than that of the Archbishop of Canterbury, was well able to look after his relatives. Francis, for example, had an income from various clerical sources of £4500 a year - a fortune in those days. This apparently included the livings of New and Old Alresford, St Mary's Southampton, Medstead and a Prebendary. He lived in the Rectory of Old Alresford and only turned up at St Cross on rent collection days.

The opportunity to line his own pockets came through the management of leases. Leases were established on the basis of an entry fine and a low annual rental. The fine was pocketed by the master. One estimate of North's peculation puts the figure at £305,700 over a 50 year period. The actual annual income required to maintain the hospital was £1,000, a figure comfortably achieved even though North was adding to his own coffers.

An example of the way this worked came from a newspaper expose in the *Hampshire Independent* in 1843. The lease of Crondale, a large property owned by the hospital became available in that year. The entry fine was £13,000, of which North received £10,706. The annual rental, which went to the hospital, was £5 a year, practically no benefit at all to the charity. The fair market rent at this time was deemed to be £2000 a year so by this means the hospital was deprived of a significant income and the potential to extend its

Above: The hospital courtyard.

Below: The interior of the Brethren Hall

On page 95: The Gatehouse and the Chapel Nave.

charitable activities. North obviously benefited as did the lessee who for six and a half years rent bought himself a lifetime interest.

The whole sorry business was brought to a conclusion through the unremitting efforts of a man called Henry Holloway, who had been appointed to the parish of St Faith, which was the local parish that used the St Cross chapel. When he discovered that something was amiss he pursued the matter and not gaining any success through representations to Francis North, by this time the Earl of Guildford, went public and the Times took up the crusade. A parliamentary enquiry was launched in 1849 and in 1851 a court case at Queen's bench led to judgement in 1853. There were still a few years to go before all was untangled but the hospital was placed into receivership. Fair leases were drawn up for the future and the master's position was established at a flat income of £250 a year with no rights over leases. The earl of Guildford was required to make limited restitution although it scarcely made a dent in his greedily acquired fortune. Anthony Trollope, the Victorian novelist, built his novel *The Warden* around this case. The earl died in 1861 with his fortune intact and at the considerable age of 89. The Times had this to say in his obituary: "All the world knows how St. Cross was for 40 years plundered by its appointed guardian."

Saint Cross

Since that time there has been not a whiff of scandal around the halls of St Cross and it can be rightly proud of its charitable purpose and its longevity. Today the charity still supports the original 13 hospital brothers of the foundation. They wear black gowns with a silver cross. The brothers from Cardinal Beaufort's bequest belong to the Order of Noble Poverty and wear claret gowns. There are 12 of them. The hospital still continues the tradition of providing bread and ale at the gatehouse for those who request

Two views of Kingsgate Street.
On page 97: The Church of St. Michael
Above right: The College West Gate
Below right: The Wykeham Arms

it. However, there is a tea room for those who would like something more appetising.

The hospital is open to visitors on most days of the year.

In common with all medieval institutions entry through a gatehouse will lead into a quadrangle. The living quarters are on the north side and as they are still inhabited you are asked to respect the privacy of the residents. Much of the hospital was rebuilt by Cardinal Beaufort in the 15th century and relatively little survives from the original 12th century building. On the eastern side is a walkway leading to the church. The

Kingsgate, at the corner of College Street and Kingsgate Street

THE OLD WYKEHAMIST BAKERY GENUINE HOME MADE BREAD

The Old Bakery on Canon Street

On page 99: Left - The Bell Inn.

Page 99; Right - Canon Street at Cuver St. corner.

upper floor was the infirmary.

The northern range to the west of the Gatehouse houses the common rooms, a hall, refectory and kitchen. They can be reached by a flight of steps.

If you need refreshment at this point there is a nice pub on the corner of the St Cross Road, the **Bell Inn (119)**.

Kingsgate Road and Street

From here walk a little way north along St Cross Road until you come to **Kingsgate Road (120)** on your right. Most of this part of Winchester was not developed until the late 19th and early 20th century but this is a pleasant suburb. Continue north until Kingsgate Road becomes Kingsgate street. This street is mostly owned by the college but many of the buildings betray their 18th century origins. Of some interest is the double fronted bow window which appears to be bulging outward in an effort to become spherical. If you take a look you will see that further expansion is restrained by iron bands.

The street of Kingsgate is almost exclusively Wykamite now, as you can see from the names on some of the houses - **Kingsgate House (121), Moberleys (122)**. Off this street eight more houses accommodate the boarders - Branston's, Sergeant's, Morshead's, Fearon's, Turner's, Du Boulay's and Chernocke House. These are lodging houses for the "commoners" attending

the school. Winchester College is exclusively a boarding school. There are no day pupils.

Most of this walk is around the perimeter of land owned by the college which has greatly expanded from its late 14th century foundation.

The **Wykeham Arms (123)** on the corner of Canon Street seems small and intimate on first entrance but expands to fill every room in the building. The walls are full of old photographs, paintings and memorabilia with college associations and the ceiling lined with hanging tankards. Some old desks have been retrieved from the college to make tables.

Canon Street

Canon Street (124) probably takes its name from the Carmelite Friars who had a friary on Kingsgate Street at one time. This land, on the east side of the street, was acquired by the

Above: Serle's House from Southgate Street

Below: The Hotel Vine

college in 1543 for expansion. It may be hard to go anywhere in Winchester without treading on ground once used by one Christian foundation or other. There were four friaries in medieval Winchester. The Austin friars had a house on Southgate Street. The Dominicans or Black Friars built at the north-eastern end of the High Street, near St. John's Hospital and the Franciscans occupied the land between Middle Brook Street and Lower Brook Street in the northern part of the city.

Canon Street is narrow but has a lot of buildings of 17th and 18th century foundation. There is a range from small terraced cottages to a few more substantial houses, many with interesting architectural ornament.

The street level has been raised several times since many of these houses were built and some houses have to step down to their ground floor. There is evidence too that some houses were shops at one time. Nicely preserved, above what was plainly a former bakery, is a painted sign advertising as much.

One large mansion, **Hamilton House (125),** on the corner of Culver Road, was built in the early 18th century by the Duke of Hamilton, reputedly as accommodation for his son while he was attending Winchester College. It seems like an awful lot for one boy. Today the house has been converted into luxury apartments.

This street is parallel to the High Street and gets steeper towards the end, but if you persevere you will come to the end of St Cross Road and the beginning of Southgate street. The actual South Gate was near to this spot, but like the other city gates was pulled down in the late 18th century to improve traffic flow.

Southgate Street

Southgate Street (126) attracted some of Winchester's grandest town houses and several on both sides are 18th century.

There are several large house here, but two on the west side can be noted.

The 18th century mansion set back from the street is known as **Serle's House (127)**. It was built in 1740 for a man called William Sheldon with a garden backing onto Southgate Street, Sheldon was a prosperous Wichester citizen who also owned the manor of East Meon. The house was acquired by James Serle in 1781 and it is from him that the house takes his name. James Serle was a prominent attorney in Winchester and often acted for the Bishop so he could well afford such a property. His descendants were closely associated with the military and in particular the Hampshire militia where they were serving officers. It was acquired in 1881 by the third battalion of the Hampshire Regiment. The house has been partly converted to a museum.

The garden just beyond has been a memorial garden to fallen soldiers since 1954. The fine 18th century mansion at the end of the garden is actually the back of Serle's hous. It fronts Gar Street an ancient street with a Sxon name. Gar usually means spear, thus Spear Street. In the past this street has been known as Bowling Green Lane and at one time was called Trafalgar Street, but the ancient name has been restored. The front of the house has a claasical pediment supported by four Tuscan colums for the entrance, although because of the rising ground the house looks less imposing from the front than it does the rear. Beyond is a grand street mansion now the **Hotel Vine (128).** It was built as a private residence in the 18th century. The original appearance appears to be intact.

Lightning Source UK Ltd.
Milton Keynes UK
UKOW06f0850280514

232440UK00002BA/28/P